2.50

From Worry to Worship

Studies in Habakkuk

by Warren W. Wiersbe
General Director
Back to the Bible Broadcast

A
BACK TO THE BIBLE
PUBLICATION
LINCOLN, NE. 68501

VICTOR BOOKS a divisi...

65,000 printed to date—1983
(5-2736—65M—123)
ISBN 0-8474-6508-X

Printed in the United States of America

Contents

Chapter 1

Meet Yourself in Habakkuk!

Have you ever looked at events in the world and wondered, What is God doing? Have you ever been perplexed about injustice, war, murder, drunkenness and a host of other problems in our sick society? Have you ever worried because of the world that you are living in? If so, then you should meet the Prophet Habakkuk. His little book of three short chapters tells us how he moved from worry to worship.

Let's get acquainted with Habakkuk and his book by asking three simple questions: Who was Habakkuk? What is the message of his book? What does this message mean to us today?

Who Was Habakkuk?

The Prophet Habakkuk was a Jewish man who lived about 600 B.C. He lived at a time when the nation of Judah was declining rapidly. It was a time of injustice, immorality and violence; it was somewhat like the world in which you and I live today. You pick up the newspapers and read reports of crime, sin and injustice. You read about terrible things happening to innocent people. And sometimes you throw up your hands and say, "Why isn't God doing something?" This was the problem Habakkuk faced. He was watching his own nation decline on the inside. But even more than that, he was watching the enemy approach from the outside. The empire of Babylon was getting strong and moving in.

When Habakkuk was serving the Lord as the prophet in Jerusalem, Jehoiakim was the king. He was the evil king who burned Jeremiah's scroll (see Jer. 36). As the Word of God was read to Jehoiakim, he took his knife and cut the scroll in pieces and burned it.

Habakkuk and Jeremiah were contemporaries in the city of Jerusalem. They had to live under the reign of an evil king. A great many false prophets were in the land, and these false prophets were promising peace. Habakkuk knew that war was coming.

Nebuchadnezzar was about to take Judah. In the year 605, Nebuchadnezzar had defeated Egypt. He was about to move in on Judah and with a series of invasions finally take the city, destroy the city and destroy the temple.

The name "Habakkuk" means *to embrace* or *to wrestle*. That's an interesting name because Habakkuk took to heart some of the serious problems of his day. As it were, he was wrestling with the Lord as he faced these problems.

Men of faith, as G. Campbell Morgan has said, are always the men who have to confront problems. Those who are not believers in God don't have to worry about these problems. If there is no God, then whatever is cannot be blamed on Him, so why worry? War is war and crime is crime, and we don't have to worry about God. But those of us who have faith in God, who believe in Jesus Christ, have to wrestle with some difficult problems. How can a God of love permit these things to happen? How can a God of justice and holiness not judge those who are doing such evil things?

Habakkuk's name means *to embrace* or *to wrestle,* and certainly he reached out to embrace God and to hold on to God, and certainly he wrestled with some serious problems: What is God doing in the world? Is there any meaning to history?

Habakkuk 3 contains a beautiful psalm, a beautiful prayer, and it is inscribed at the end "To the chief singer on my stringed instruments" (v. 19). This notation indicates that Habakkuk may have been a levitical priest, because the psalm is written as if it belonged to the levitical choir in the temple. So it's possible that, like Jeremiah, Habakkuk had begun as a priest and been called to become a prophet.

That would be a difficult thing, wouldn't it? A priest lived a rather routine life. A priest knew what he was going to do every day. He had a calendar, he had a guidebook—Exodus and Leviticus—and he knew exactly what to do, how to handle the sacrifices, how to mix the incense, how to burn the sacrifices, how to take care of the temple. A priest lived a rather routine life, but a prophet didn't. A priest had a very secure, safe life, but a prophet didn't.

God called Habakkuk at a time when his nation needed to hear the Word of God, and Habakkuk ceased to be a priest and became a prophet.

What Was Habakkuk's Message?

Question number two: What is the message of his book? It's a very small book; it's one of the minor prophets, but it has a major message. Habakkuk was dealing with the age-old problem of evil in the world.

My library contains a number of books written by philosophers dealing with the problem of evil. How do you explain evil in this world if we believe in a God of love and justice?

Wondering and Worrying

The little Book of Habakkuk is put together in a beautiful way. In chapter 1 the prophet was *wondering* and *worrying*. He had three accusations against God. Accusation number one was God is *indifferent*. "O Lord, how long shall I cry? I've been praying, and You're not doing anything" (see Hab. 1:2). God is indifferent.

Then he asked, "Why dost thou show me iniquity, and cause me to behold grievance? For spoiling and violence are before me; and there are those who raise up strife and contention. Therefore, the law is slacked, and justice doth never go forth; for the wicked doth compass about the righteous; therefore, justice goeth forth perverted"(vv. 3,4). He said that God is not only indifferent, God is *inactive*; He's not doing anything.

God answered him in verses 5-11: "I am working. I'm doing a work so wonderful you will not believe it. I'm going to raise up the Babylonians, and they will come and chasten My people and take them into captivity." That raised another problem, and Habakkuk accused God of being *inconsistent* (vv. 12-17). How could a holy God use such a wicked nation as the Babylonians to punish the people of Israel?

So in chapter 1 you find the prophet was down in the valley. Oh, he was so low! He thought that God was indifferent, inactive and inconsistent.

Before we criticize him, let's confess that sometimes *we* have made the same accusations against God. We've said, "God, how long am I going to have to pray about this? How long am I going to have to talk to You about this? Are You indifferent to my prayers? God, are You inactive? Why are these things happening? Why are the righteous suffering while the ungodly seem to be prospering? God, You are inconsistent."

How do you solve these problems? Some people say, "Well, I just won't believe in God anymore." Of course, we can't do that because we know that God is real, that our Father is in heaven. The Lord Jesus Christ made it very real and very personal to us when He said, "He that hath seen me hath seen the Father" (John 14:9). So we know that God is real. We cannot deny the reality of God.

Neither can we deny the reality of evil. Some people do that. They say, "Well, what looks like evil is not really evil at all; it's just the figment of your imagination. Evil is not something real; it's just error in your mind." Habakkuk didn't do that. He knew that the evil he saw was very real.

Watching and Waiting

What did he do? In Habakkuk 2 he got up into his watchtower. "I will stand upon my watch, and set myself upon the tower" (v. 1). He was getting a little higher now. He got out of the valley where he'd been wondering and worrying, and he went up into the watchtower to begin watching and waiting. He said, "I'm going to watch and see what God will say to me. God's going to answer me," and God did answer him.

God answered him in an amazing way. In Habakkuk 2 you find five woes. "Woe to him that increaseth that which is not his!"—selfish ambition (v. 6). "Woe to him that coveteth an evil covetousness to his house"—covetousness (v. 9). "Woe to him that buildeth a town with blood"—woe upon those who exploit others (v. 12). "Woe unto him that giveth his neighbor drink"—woe upon the drunkards and those who promote drunkenness (v. 15). "Woe unto him that saith to the wood, Awake; to the dumb stone, Arise, it shall teach!"—woe to idolaters (v. 19).

Here we have the dark background of five woes. These were the sins of the people. These were the sins of the people of Judah, Habakkuk's own people. These were also the sins of the Babylonians who were going to swoop down upon Judah and take the people captive.

These are the sins of nations today—greed,

plunder, covetousness, murder, drunkenness and idolatry. It's a miracle that God doesn't swoop down upon every nation, because these are the sins of people today.

Against this dark background of woe, God gave Habakkuk three very marvelous assurances (vv. 4,14,20). These are the stars that shine in the night of God's judgment.

First, there is the assurance of *God's grace.* "Behold, his soul that is lifted up is not upright in him; but the just shall live by his faith" (v. 4). The first assurance is the assurance of God's grace. "If you will trust Me, in My grace I will work everything out."

"For the earth shall be filled with the knowledge of the glory of the Lord, as the waters cover the sea"—the assurance of *God's glory* (v. 14). God was saying, "Habakkuk, as you look out from your watchtower, all you see is drunkenness, greed, covetousness, murder and idolatry. But I want you to know that the day is coming when the earth is going to be filled with the knowledge of the glory of the Lord, as the waters cover the sea." This is the assurance of God's glory.

Meanwhile, what should we do? "But the Lord is in his holy temple; let all the earth keep silence before him"—the assurance of *God's government* (v. 20). God said, "Habakkuk, I am on the throne. Everything is in My control; so do not worry and fret."

We need these assurances today. I pick up my morning newspaper, and I see reports of greed and plunder and immorality and idolatry, reports of drunkenness and murder—all kinds of wickedness. I put the paper down and say, "Why doesn't God do something?" But God says to me, "I *am* doing something. Lay hold of My assurances. The assurance of My grace—live by faith, not by sight. The assurance of My glory—one day this earth shall be covered with glory. The assurance of My government—I am in My holy temple. Now just keep quiet. 'Be still, and know that I am God' (Ps. 46:10)."

Worshiping and Witnessing

In Habakkuk 3 we see a transformation in the life of Habakkuk. He has moved from wondering and worrying down in the valley (ch. 1) to watching and waiting up in the watchtower (ch. 2) to worshiping and witnessing as he runs upon the mountaintop (ch. 3). It's an amazing thing! The book ends in verse 19, "He will make me walk upon mine high places." The book didn't start with high places, did it? It started down in the valley where he could hardly believe that God really cared.

So in chapter 3 we have the prophet worshiping and witnessing. He began by *praying*, "Revive thy work in the midst of the years" (v. 2). "Lord, keep Your work going. I believe that You are working now. Keep it going. Fulfill Your promise." "In wrath remember mercy" (v. 2). That's the grace of God. So in verses 1 and 2 the prophet was *praying*.

In verses 3-16 the prophet was *pondering*. He was pondering the ways of the Lord. We have a beautiful poetic description of the power of God, the acts of

God in history. The prophet looked back and realized that in past years God had kept His promises, God had saved His people, God had given victory. He knew God could help the nation again.

Then in verses 17-19 you find the prophet *praising*. "Although the fig tree shall not blossom, neither shall fruit be in the vines," and he went on to say, though everything may fail, "I will rejoice in the Lord, I will joy in the God of my salvation. The Lord God is my strength, and he will make my feet like hinds' feet [swift and sure], and he will make me walk upon mine high places." The prophet ended in a place of victory, didn't he, because he learned to trust in the Lord?

What Is the Message for Us?

What is the main message of this book for us today? Let me summarize it like this: When you live by faith, you aren't worried about the things that go on in the world. You may be burdened. It doesn't mean we shouldn't be concerned about crime and injustice, but we don't lose our faith because of it. We don't become discouraged and despondent and give up. The main message of Habakkuk is that the just shall live by faith. Believe God's Word. Believe that God's purposes will be fulfilled, and you will move from the valley to the mountaintop of victory and blessing.

Habakkuk teaches us that God permits evil in the world. But God uses evil in His own way, and eventually God will judge evil, triumph over evil and bring His glory to pass. We need to know that.

There are many things in this life we don't understand; we can't explain them. We can't explain sickness or accidents or murder. We can't explain why godly people suffer. There is no clear explanation. But we don't live by *explanations*, we live by *promises.* The just shall live by faith. God does permit evil in this world, but God uses it to accomplish His own purposes, and one day God will judge evil and triumph over it.

Habakkuk teaches us how to go from worry to worship, from the valley to the watchtower to the mountaintop; from sighing (ch. 1) to silence (ch. 2) to singing (ch. 3) where he rejoiced in the blessing of the Lord.

Habakkuk was a marvelous man, a man who wrestled with some serious problems and won the victory. And that victory can be yours today if you'll learn the great lesson of the Prophet Habakkuk—the just shall live by faith.

Chapter 2

God, Aren't You Listening?

(Hab. 1:1-4)

Some Christians go through life with their eyes closed. They live in a fool's paradise as they carelessly ignore what is really going on in the world. The Prophet Habakkuk was not that kind of a person. When you open the Bible to Habakkuk 1:1, you read: "The burden which Habakkuk, the prophet, did see." He said to God, "Why dost thou show me iniquity?" (v. 3). He also said, "I will stand upon my watch, and set myself upon the tower, and will watch to see what he will say unto me" (2:1).

The Prophet Habakkuk was a man with open eyes, and because he was a man with open eyes, he was a man with a burdened heart. "The burden which Habakkuk, the prophet, did see" (1:1).

We discovered that in chapter 1, the Prophet Habakkuk was *wondering and worrying.* He was wondering and worrying because as he looked out on his nation, he saw wickedness and sin. The nation of Judah was in decline—politically, economically, morally and spiritually. They had rejected the

Word of the Lord, and sin was rampant in the nation of Judah.

Outside the nation, the Babylonian empire was on the move. God was showing Habakkuk that Babylon was going to come and conquer Judah. The people would go into captivity. His nation was going to suffer greatly.

The Prophet Habakkuk was a man who was perplexed. He didn't quite understand what God was doing. And so he did what all of us must do when we are perplexed—he took the problem to God. He didn't turn to some philosopher; he didn't look for advice from some ungodly people; he simply went to God and said, "God, I have problems." In fact, as Habakkuk wrestled with his problems, he made three accusations against God.

First Accusation: Indifference

First, he accused God of being indifferent. "O Lord, how long shall I cry, and thou wilt not hear! Even cry out unto thee of violence, and thou wilt not save!" (Hab. 1:2). How many times have you and I said, "Lord, how long?" You find this prayer many times in the Book of Psalms. "How long must I cry out, O Lord? How long will evil prosper?" Throughout the ages, the saints of God have looked at the world with all of its wickedness and said, "O Lord Jesus, how long?"

You will notice that Habakkuk was praying very fervently. "How long shall I cry?" That first word "*cry*" means "to cry for help." He was crying out for the help of God. "O God, help me and help my nation." "How long shall I cry, and thou wilt not hear!" (v. 2).

Have you ever prayed fervently for help, and it seemed as though God did not hear? Even the disciples had a problem like that, didn't they? "Lord, don't You care that we are perishing?" (see Mark 4:38). Sometimes we pray and we cry and we wonder why God doesn't say something or do something.

The second time Habakkuk used the word "*cry*" in verse 2, it means "to scream." "Even cry [scream] out unto thee of violence, and thou wilt not save!"

Six times in his little book Habakkuk used the word "violence." He was living in a time when society was falling apart. Jeremiah lived in that same time. They were watching the internal decay of their nation. I wonder if we are living in a similar period in history. We are seeing immorality and injustice and indecency triumph. It seems as if those who believe in that which is good are on the scaffold and those who believe in that which is evil are too often on the throne.

Habakkuk was praying fervently, crying for help, screaming out to God, and yet he seemed to get no answer to his prayer. What was he praying about? He was praying about the sins of his people. He realized that the nation was falling apart. He was praying for revival. He was praying that God's people would get stirred up, that they would wake up and clean up and stand up against that which was wrong. But God did not answer. God apparently was indifferent. "Thou wilt not save!" (v. 2).

Second Accusation: Inactivity

And then in Habakkuk 1:3,4 he had a second accusation against God. Not only was God indifferent, but *God was inactive*. Here the question was not "How long?" but "Why?"

"Why?" is a difficult question to answer sometimes. Little children come to their parents and say, "Why is the sky blue? Why is the grass green?" It's not easy to answer all of these questions. But those are easy questions compared to questions like this: "Why dost thou show me iniquity, and cause me to behold grievance? For spoiling and violence are before me; and there are those who raise up strife and contention. Therefore, the law is slacked, and justice doth never go forth; for the wicked doth compass about the righteous; therefore, justice goeth forth perverted" (vv. 3,4). In other words, he was saying, "God, You are inactive. Why don't You judge the sins of the people?"

I know people don't like preachers to talk about sin. They want us to talk about other things, but sometimes we have to point out sin.

Josiah had been the king until 608 B.C., and he had issued orders for reformation. They had found the Law in the temple, and having read the Law, they realized how wicked they were, "for by the law is the knowledge of sin" (Rom. 3:20). Josiah had brought about a great reformation. The temple had been restored, the idols had been removed and destroyed, the wicked people in the land had been dealt with. There had been a great reformation.

But reformation without repentance and regeneration never lasts. The Law can reveal sin, and the Law can rebuke sin, but the Law cannot change the heart. You can issue a law against idolatry and remove all the idols, but you'll never change the idols that are in people's hearts.

Josiah had led a marvelous reform, but it was superficial. It was not lasting; it was shallow. I'm not saying it was wrong; I'm just saying it was temporary. The men and women of Judah had gone back to their sins again.

Habakkuk named these sins. One was *violence*—we've seen that in Habakkuk 1:2, and it's again repeated in verse 3. Has there ever been a time when we've seen so much violence? I can remember that as a little child I could walk the streets of the city where I lived, and I felt perfectly safe. I could go to the park and the swimming pool and not feel threatened. Today you can hardly walk out of your house without wondering if somebody is going to drive by and do something to you. Violence!

Another sin Habakkuk mentioned was *iniquity*. The word "iniquity" means vanity. It means that the ungodly are prospering. Those who don't believe in the Word of God and don't want to do the will of God are succeeding. Those who are wicked are seemingly prospering and making progress. Those who try to do the will of God are suffering.

The prophet also mentioned *grievance*—it means misery. The people were being exploited. The poor were being exploited by the rich. Those out of office were being exploited by those who were in office.

The people were experiencing *spoiling*—that means destruction. The family was being destroyed. Homes were being destroyed. The nation was being destroyed. Foundations were shaking. "*Strife*" refers to disputes and fightings. It goes along with *contention.* Strife and contention—that's a description of society today. The Republicans are against the Democrats, the blacks and the whites disagree, the rich and the poor disagree. The *ins* and the *outs* fight. Strife and contention.

Habakkuk also listed the sin of *injustice.* The Law was slack. The Hebrew word means *paralyzed.* The Law was paralyzed. The Law could do nothing. Today we have more lawyers and more courts and more judges and more laws—and more lawlessness! The lawyers themselves admit that our legal system is paralyzed. Sometimes it takes years for a case to even be settled.

The law is paralyzed. "Justice doth never go forth" (v. 4). The law is also *perverted.* "Therefore, justice goeth forth perverted" (v. 4). It is possible for lawyers or judges or even common people like you and me to twist the law to make it mean anything we desire!

Habakkuk lived at a period of time that seems very much like our own. He said, "God is indifferent. How long shall I cry out? God, why don't You do something? Why do You show me these things and yet do nothing about them?" That's a good question. Why doesn't God just send fire from heaven and burn up all the wicked people? Because it wouldn't change anything. We could have reformation, but we need regeneration. Hearts have to be changed.

You don't change the problems just by changing people in office. The heart of every problem is the problem in the heart, and until the heart is changed by grace, society will not change at all.

Why doesn't God do something? Let me remind you—*sometimes God lets us get exactly what we deserve*. People don't want the Bible, they don't want Gospel-preaching churches, they don't want standards, they don't want absolutes, they don't want the Ten Commandments. God says, "Fine, if you don't want them, you can have what you want." And they get the consequences of rejecting God's way.

It never ceases to amaze me how politicians want all the *fruit* of the Gospel but not the *roots* of the Gospel. They don't want the Bible, they don't want prayer, they don't want morality, but they do want honesty—they want people to pay their taxes. They do want justice. But you can't have honesty and justice and all the things that make up a good society without hearts that are in submission to God. "The fear of the Lord is the beginning of wisdom" (Prov. 9:10).

God appeared to be inactive. God was permitting the people of Judah to reap exactly what they had sown. They had supported idolatrous worship, and they got the results of it. They had neglected the spiritual teaching of the temple, and they got the results of it. The people of Judah wanted false peace and false prosperity, and they got the results of it.

Third Accusation: Inconsistency

The third accusation that Habakkuk made was that God is *inconsistent* (see Hab. 1:5-17). We'll be studying this section in greater detail in the next chapter. But God said to Habakkuk, "Look, I am not indifferent, I'm concerned. I'm not inactive, I'm working." "Behold among the nations, and regard, and wonder marvelously; for I will work a work in your days, which ye will not believe, though it be told you" (v. 5). What was the work God was going to do? God was going to raise up the Chaldeans, and they were going to swoop down upon Judah and wipe it clean, the way a man wipes a plate.

This created a third problem for Habakkuk. It was bad enough to accuse God of being indifferent and inactive, but then he said, "God, You are *inconsistent*." "Art thou not from everlasting, O Lord, my God, mine Holy One? . . . Thou art of purer eyes than to behold evil, and canst not look [in favor] on iniquity" (vv. 12,13). In other words, "God, You are inconsistent. How can You use a nation more wicked than we are to punish us? We are Your covenant people. They are outsiders. We have at least tried in some measure to serve You. They have rebelled against You. How can You use a wicked nation to punish Your people Judah?"

These three accusations are heard today. In my own pastoral ministry I've had people come to me and say, "I don't think God cares anymore." I recall stepping into a hospital room one day where a dear lady was lying in the bed in great pain, and she said,

"Oh, Pastor, I don't think God cares about me anymore." I reminded her that the Word of God says, "Casting all your care upon him; for he careth for you" (I Pet. 5:7). She said, "Yes, I know that's in the Word, but it's so hard to believe it just now."

God sometimes seems to be indifferent, and God sometimes seems to be inactive. Why doesn't God do something? Why doesn't God get me a job? Why doesn't God heal my body? Why doesn't God save my wayward son? Why doesn't God put our home together? Why doesn't God do something about the pornography and the wickedness in our city? Why doesn't God do something? And God comes back and says, "I'm working, I'm working."

Remember, the key idea in Habakkuk is found in 2:4: "The just shall live by his faith." We should not live by sight. It's good to have our eyes open. It's good to look around and see what's going on. But we shouldn't interpret what we see from a human point of view. To walk by faith means to look at earth from heaven's point of view. To walk by sight means to look at heaven from earth's point of view.

God is not indifferent, and God is not inactive, and God is not inconsistent. He is a holy God, He is a righteous God. He knows what He is doing. Habakkuk needed to claim Romans 8:28, didn't he? "And we know that all things work together for good to them that love God, to them who are the called according to his purpose." Habakkuk didn't have the Book of Romans, but he did have the God of the Book of Romans. And before this little prophecy ended, Habakkuk was rejoicing in the

Lord. He moved from wondering and worrying to worshiping and witnessing.

Where does this find you today? Do you think that God is indifferent? Are you crying out, "Why? How long? How can You do this?" Do you think that God is inactive or that God is inconsistent? Then I would say to you, "Do what Habakkuk did. Walk by faith."

You're going to discover in chapter 2 that Habakkuk went into his watchtower and waited to see what God would say to him. God said, "Habakkuk, don't worry. Live by faith. One day My glory shall fill this world. Meanwhile, the Lord is in His holy temple. Let all the earth keep silence before Him. Be still, and know that I am God."

Chapter 3

An Amazing Work

(Hab. 1:5-11)

The Prophet Habakkuk asked God two important questions: "How long?" and "Why?" Each of us has asked these questions at one time or another. Habakkuk 1:2 says, "O Lord, how long shall I cry, and thou wilt not hear!" It was the problem of God's indifference. Habakkuk was wondering, "Why isn't God listening to me? Why isn't God answering me? Certainly God can see all the violence and all the sin that is going on in the nation." In verse 3 he asked the question why: "Why dost thou show me iniquity, and cause me to behold grievance?" Habakkuk asked God, "Why am I allowed to see these things, and why are You not doing something?" God not only seemed indifferent to the Prophet Habakkuk, but God seemed to be inactive. He was not listening, and He was not working.

You may be feeling that way today. It may be that you are praying about something—some important situation, some problem—and yet God doesn't seem to hear, and God doesn't seem to work. God's ear seems to be deaf, and God's hand seems to be paralyzed.

God answered these questions in Habakkuk 1:5-11. He said, "I am not indifferent, I am not inactive. I am at work accomplishing My purpose in this world." God gave Habakkuk, and us, two descriptions of the situation over which He had control. First He described *His work* in verses 5 and 6, and then He described *His workers* in verses 7-11.

God's Work

First of all, *God described His work*. What was God doing? "Behold among the nations, and regard, and wonder marvelously: for I will work a work in your days, which ye will not believe, though it be told you. For, lo, I raise up the Chaldeans, that bitter and hasty nation, which shall march through the breadth of the land, to possess the dwelling places that are not theirs" (Hab. 1:5,6).

Amazing and Unbelievable

God gave a *revelation* here of His work. He did not give an *explanation* of all that He was doing, but He gave a revelation. What He said here is simply this: "Habakkuk, I am doing something so amazing, so marvelous and so wonderful that if I did explain it to you, you wouldn't understand it. In fact, you're going to have a hard time believing it."

This is an important principle. God's work is amazing. God's work is unbelievable. Therefore, God does not always explain things to us. God tells us as much as we can take and as much as we can understand. Jesus said to His disciples, "I have many things to say to you, but you cannot bear them now" (see John 16:12). Each of us is at a different level in our spiritual life, and God knows where we are. God knows what we can take. You can't tell your children some things because they are not ready to receive them.

This is the answer to those who say, "Why? How long? God, explain things to me." We do not live by explanations; we live by promises. God explained to Habakkuk just as much as he could take. He explains to us just as much as we can take. He does this to encourage us because we do not live on explanations, we live on promises.

Why doesn't God give us detailed explanations of His work? Well, for two reasons. The first reason is that we could not understand all of it to begin with. God's ways are above our ways. God's thoughts are beyond our thoughts. It's not important that I understand all about God. In fact, I could not worship a God I completely understood. God has to be above me and beyond me. Life has to have its mysteries. Your life cannot be like some machine, every wheel and cog of which you can explain. Life must have its mystery if it is going to have its adventure. If we're going to live by faith, then we cannot rest only on explanations.

The second reason why God does not tell us everything about His work is simply this: We wouldn't believe it anyway. That's what He tells us. "Which ye will not believe, though it be told you" (Hab. 1:5).

Our tendency, whenever God explains something to us, is to argue with Him. Peter did this. Our

Lord began to explain to His disciples that He was going to go to Jerusalem to die, and what did Peter do with this explanation? He refuted it. He argued with it. He got the Lord off to one side and said, "Far be it from You, Lord! Pity Yourself! This shall not happen to You" (see Matt. 16:22). Jesus looked at Peter and turned and said, "Get thee behind me, Satan (adversary). You are not thinking like God, you're thinking like a man" (see v. 23).

This is the problem, isn't it? If God did explain things to you—why you are in the hospital, why the baby died, why your husband lost his job, why your son had an auto accident—would it make you a better person? Would you really love the Lord more and trust Him more, having had this explanation? I don't think so. Explanations do not encourage faith—promises do.

As I read the life of Abraham, that great man of faith, I notice that God explained very little to him. God did not give him long, detailed explanations, blueprints, guidebooks. *He gave him promises.* In fact, Abraham began his life of faith holding on to that great promise that he would have a son, and through him all the nations of the earth would be blessed.

Deliberate and Diligent

God described His work as an amazing work and an unbelievable work and as a very *deliberate* work. I notice that the Hebrew word translated *work* in Habakkuk 1:5 means "the diligent work of a man at his trade." It's the word used for a carpenter who is carefully making a piece of furniture or a potter who is carefully molding a jar. God's work is an amazing work, an unbelievable work and a deliberate and diligent work. God is at work *carefully*. He's taking care of all the details. That's why we can quote Romans 8:28 with confidence: "And we know that all things work together for good to them that love God, to them who are the called according to his purpose." God is working *completely*—all things. God is working *constantly*—all things are working together for good. God is working *coherently*, putting *everything* together to accomplish His purposes.

So God's work is a deliberate, diligent work. He knows what He is doing. And God's work is a necessary work. God didn't ask for permission to do anything. God didn't come to Habakkuk and say, "Let's take a vote. Do you think I should do this?" God does what is necessary. God knows what needs to be done.

His work is described in Habakkuk 1:6. He was going to raise up the Babylonians to punish the Jews. In the Old Testament, you'll find that God often used the Gentiles to punish the Jews. Different nations came into the Holy Land and punished the Jewish people during the period of the Book of Judges. But now God was going to take them *out of their land* and take them to Babylon. He described the Chaldeans as a bitter (ruthless) and hasty (impetuous) nation. The Chaldeans were not friendly to other nations. They were a ruthless nation. They tortured, they killed, they plundered. They were a rash and impetuous nation. They rushed through to get the job done.

"Which shall march through the breadth of the land" (v. 6). That word "march" means "to sweep through." This was not going to be some little raid; this was going to be a complete invasion. The Babylonians would be victorious.

Daniel 7:4 describes Babylon as a lion with wings. Habakkuk was going to find out about that, wasn't he? A lion with wings—ruthless and impetuous, hasty, speeding along, killing as they went.

God told Habakkuk, "This is My work, and I'm going to do it. I will do it carefully and deliberately, and I will do it lovingly. You don't think it's going to be a good thing for the people of your land, but it is. The Jewish people need what is coming from the Babylonians" (see Hab. 1:6).

God's Workers

In Habakkuk 1:7-11 God described *His workers*. God uses all kinds of workers to accomplish His purposes. He can use saved people and unsaved people. He can use individuals or nations. God is sovereign, and He is in charge of the nations. The rise and fall of the nations is in His hands.

In Acts 17:26 we read: "[He] hath made of one blood all nations of men to dwell on all the face of the earth." So God made the nations. And He "hath determined the times before appointed" (v. 26). God's in charge of history. "And the bounds of their habitation" (v. 26)—God is in charge of geography. God is in charge of the nations. This does not mean that God is to be blamed for what the nations do. It does mean that God is completely sovereign. He establishes one nation. He allows another nation's downfall.

On God's calendar it was time for Babylon to emerge as a great world power. God gave two descriptions of the Babylonian nation. In Habakkuk 1:7,8 He compared them to *animals*, and in verses 9 and 10 He compared them to *a desert wind*. Each of these descriptions would be very meaningful to the people who would listen to Habakkuk's prophecy.

Like Animals

In Habakkuk 1:7,8 God said, "My workers are like ravaging animals. Their horses also are swifter than the leopards." That's pretty swift! "And are more fierce than the evening wolves." The soldiers would be fierce, but even the horses are fierce!

Here we have horses, leopards and wolves. In other words, God was saying, "When the Babylonians come, it won't be men attacking men, it will be *animals* attacking men."

It's interesting to note that in the Bible men and women who do not live for God are often compared to animals. In Psalm 32:9 God said to David, "Be ye not like the horse, or like the mule." When David went out to commit adultery with Bathsheba, he was acting like an animal.

Proverbs 7:22,23 gives the description of a young man who's about to go off with a harlot, and it says that he's going like an animal to the slaughter. "He goeth after her straightway, as an ox goeth to the slaughter, or as a fool to the correction of the stocks, till an arrow strike through his liver—as a bird hasteneth to the snare, and knoweth not that it is for his life." Here's a young man ready to commit fornication, and God says that when you live like that, you're living like an animal, like an ox going to the slaughter.

The Babylonians were fearful and dreadful. "Their horsemen shall spread themselves, and their horsemen shall come from far; they shall fly like the eagle that hasteth to eat" (Hab. 1:8). As I mentioned before, Daniel 7:4 describes the Babylonian nation as a lion with wings. So here we have horses and leopards and wolves and eagles. "They shall come all for violence" (Hab. 1:9). They are bent on destruction. "The set of their faces is forward" (v. 9). They just keep advancing, keep moving. "And they shall gather the captives as the sand" (v. 9).

Like the Desert Wind

In Habakkuk 1:9,10 God changed the picture from animals to that of the desert wind. Verse 9 can be translated, "They advance like a desert wind." The desert wind is hot and uncomfortable. It just keeps on blowing. The desert wind is devastating. It can smother you. Just as the wind blows on the desert, just as the wind keeps moving forward, shifting all that sand, so the armies of the Babylonians were going to come, and nothing was going to stop them. "They shall scoff at the kings" (v. 10). The Babylonians used to capture the kings alive and put them in cages and exhibit them like animals at a zoo. "And the princes shall be a scorn unto them; they shall deride every stronghold" (v. 10). The people of Judah could put up all that they wanted to put up to protect themselves, but it was not going to stop them. The Babylonians laughed at every stronghold, "for they shall heap dust, and take it" (v. 10). They could build earthen ramps to get into the city. Another translation says, "They sweep past like the wind and go on—guilty men, whose strength is their god" (v. 11, NIV).

The desert wind, the violent animals is God's picture of His workers. You say, "How can God use people like this to accomplish His purposes?" Can God use the blast of war? Yes. Can God use the violence of animallike people? Yes, He can. Verse 11 tells me that the Babylonians honored their strength. Their god was power. "Then shall his mind change, and he shall pass over, and offend, imputing this his power unto his god" (v. 11). In other words, they said their strength was their god. "Our god is the god of power. The God of Abraham, Isaac and Jacob cannot stop us."

It's interesting to note that Habakkuk 1:5 is quoted in Acts 13:38-41. Paul quoted this to the people in the synagogue. He stated that God is doing a work, and we had better heed what God is doing. Acts 13:40,41 says, "Beware, therefore, lest that come upon you, which is spoken of in the prophets; Behold, ye despisers, and wonder, and perish; for I work a work in your days, a work which ye shall in no way believe, though a man declare it unto you."

In Habakkuk's day God used the Gentiles to punish the Jews, but now in this day—the day of the Gospel—God is using the Jews to win the Gentiles. Here was Paul, a Jew, preaching to Jews and Gentiles. God was doing a great work in Paul's day, and God is still doing that great work. This is the day of salvation. It's wonderful, isn't it, that God is today saving Jews and Gentiles and forming one Body, the Church? Don't despise the work of God, because today is the day of salvation.

God knows what He is doing. He is not indifferent. He is not inactive. He knows what His work is. He can use whatever instruments He wants to use. He will achieve His purposes. Just remember, the just shall live by faith.

Chapter 4

God, Are You Making a Mistake?

(Hab. 1:12-17)

God answered the prophet's questions. Habakkuk asked, "Why? How long?" and God answered him. But the answer that God gave only created more problems and raised more serious questions in the heart of Habakkuk. It was bad enough that God seemed indifferent and inactive, but now He appeared to be inconsistent.

How could a holy God use a wicked nation like Babylon to punish the people of Judah who were, after all, God's covenant people? As Habakkuk wrestled with this seeming inconsistency on the part of God, he argued with God. He presented three arguments to God and tried to convince God to change His mind.

Before you criticize Habakkuk for doing this, how many times have we done the same thing? How many times have we thought that God was inconsistent? We see the ungodly prospering and the godly suffering. We see the children of the ungodly, the unbelieving, experiencing health and blessing, and yet our own children sometimes suffer sickness and trials.

Habakkuk was wrestling with God. His name means "the wrestler, the embracer." How could God allow Babylon to come upon the people of Judah?

Habakkuk presented three arguments. In Habakkuk 1:12,13—*the holiness of God*; verses 14 and 15—*the helplessness of the people*; and verses 16 and 17—*the haughtiness of the enemy*. In other words, God seemed to be violating His own holiness. He seemed to be adding to the helplessness of His people, and He seemed to be promoting the pride and haughtiness of the enemy.

The Holiness of God

Habakkuk 1:12,13 gives us Habakkuk's first argument—*the holiness of God*. This is really a digest of theology. Habakkuk, the prophet, was a good theologian. He knew what God was like. "Art thou not from everlasting, O Lord, my God, mine Holy One?" (v. 12).

God Is Eternal

The first thing Habakkuk noticed was that *God is the eternal God*. This means that God is not caught by surprise. Eternity is not time lengthened out; eternity is that realm in which God lives. God is eternal. God is not controlled by time. God is not limited by time. We're told in II Peter 3:8 that a thousand years with God is as one day and that one day is as a thousand years. Therefore, we must not limit God in terms of time. What God does in time is a part of His eternal plan.

Habakkuk said, "You are an eternal God. You are not caught by surprise. You knew that this was going to happen because You had plans and decrees" (see Hab. 1:12). That's why he went on to say, "We shall not die. O Lord, thou hast ordained them for judgment" (v. 12). In other words, God works by His own plan. Since God is eternal and since God had made His covenants with the people of Israel, He was going to keep His promise. God had agreed to watch over the nation. God had agreed that through the nation all the nations of the earth would be blessed. "Therefore," Habakkuk said, "we shall not die. We are not going to be exterminated. Whatever happens, You have ordained, O Lord."

Some people don't like this kind of theology. They want to exalt mankind. But I think that the prophets knew better. In fact, all who wrote in the Word of God exalted the sovereignty of God. God is free because God is eternal.

God Is Unchanging

Second, *God is unchanging.* "And, O Mighty God, thou hast established them for correction" (Hab. 1:12). The little phrase "Mighty God" literally means "O rock." It refers back to Deuteronomy 32:4 where God is called the rock.

Why would Habakkuk call God a rock? A rock is

unchanging. A rock pictures stability, security and continuity. So God is unchanging. And since He is the Lord (meaning Jehovah, the covenant-making God), He has His unchanging purposes and His unchanging promises.

It is a great encouragement to know that God is eternal in times of trial and testing. Nothing catches Him by surprise. God is unchanging. He's not going to change in His attitude toward us. He's not going to change in His character. His promises are not going to change. Whatever He ordains is going to be worked out.

God Is Holy, or Pure

Then in Habakkuk 1:13 Habakkuk reminded God of His own holiness—*the holiness of God.* God is called the Holy One in verse 12. "Thou art of purer eyes than to behold evil, and canst not look on iniquity" (v. 13). Don't misinterpret that phrase. He's not saying that God doesn't *see* sin. Of course God sees sin. Nothing is hidden from "the eyes of him with whom we have to do" (Heb. 4:13). God sees all things. He sees the thoughts and the intents of our hearts (see v. 12). What this means is that God cannot look *with approval* on sin. God cannot behold evil and approve of it. His eyes are pure. His heart is pure. Therefore, Habakkuk was arguing, "How can You look upon these Babylonians, who are such wicked people, and approve what they are doing? How can You use an unholy instrument to accomplish a holy purpose?"

Habakkuk was wrestling with a real problem of theology. But he forgot that God's ways are above our ways and that God's thoughts are above our thoughts. It's true that God does judge sin. It is true that God does not look with favor upon sin. But it is also true that God sent His Son to die for our sins. God settled the sin problem once and for all at Calvary. He settled the sin problem when His Son died on the cross. All sin has efficiently and effectively been dealt with at the cross of Jesus Christ. Therefore, God is free to handle sinners as He wishes. No one can ever say to God, "You allowed a sin to get by." No, every sin has been dealt with on the cross of Calvary.

This is why the prophet said, "We shall not die. O Lord, thou hast ordained them for judgment; and, O Mighty God, thou hast established them for correction" (Hab. 1:12). God can even use the wicked Chaldeans to correct and discipline His people.

I've noticed often in the Scriptures that God humbles His sinning people by using other sinful people to discipline them. When Abraham got out of the will of God and went to Egypt, he was embarrassed and rebuked by a heathen king (see Gen. 12:10-20). Pharaoh rebuked Abraham in the presence of many people.

I note in the Book of Judges that when the people of Israel sinned against God, He brought in the Philistines and the Midianites and other pagan nations to discipline them and to rebuke them for their sin.

The Prophet Habakkuk asked, "Why lookest thou upon them that deal treacherously, and holdest thy tongue when the wicked devoureth the man that is more righteous than he?" (Hab. 1:13). He was concerned because God was silent. "Why doesn't God say something? Why doesn't He judge the wicked?"

People down through the centuries have been concerned about the silence of God. We do not hear voices from heaven. God does not send immediate judgment upon wicked nations today. God is allowing the wickedness of people, gradually, quietly, to bring about its own judgment. God says, "All right, I'm just going to let you alone. If you want to go in that direction, go right ahead. But I want you to know that your sin is going to find you out."

One day God will effectively judge this world. One day Jesus Christ shall return "in flaming fire taking vengeance on them that know not God, and that obey not the gospel of our Lord Jesus Christ" (II Thess. 1:8). But meanwhile, the heavens are silent. Why are the heavens silent today? Because God's last word was spoken through Jesus Christ (see Heb. 1:1,2). God no longer necessarily speaks to us in voices from heaven or in thunder or earthquakes. He is speaking to us through His Son. The greatest word He ever spoke was at Calvary.

Habakkuk looked at the holiness of God and said, "God, I can't believe that a holy God would allow this to happen." Notice that Habakkuk called Him "My God, mine Holy One" (Hab. 1:12). He had not lost his faith. He still believed that God was his own Saviour.

The Helplessness of the People

Habakkuk's first argument concerned the holiness of God. His second argument was *the helplessness of the people.* He compared the people of Judah and the people who were being attacked by Babylon to fish. God had compared Babylon to animals, but Habakkuk the prophet said, "We are as helpless as fish." "And makest men as the fish of the sea, as the creeping things, that have no ruler over them?" (Hab. 1:14). We're like fish and reptiles. We are just nothing. We have no protection whatsoever. "They take up all of them with the hook; they catch them in their net, and gather them in their drag; therefore, they rejoice and are glad" (v. 15). He saw the people who were being taken by Babylon as fish who are helpless, without protection. The hook illustrated the catching of individuals; the nets illustrated the catching of groups of people. He was saying, "O God, Your people are so helpless."

I'm not much of a fisherman. And it seems to me that sometimes the fish are smarter than the fishermen. But the picture here is a vivid one. Great dragnets swoop down upon the schools of fish and catch them, and the fish are helpless and cannot get away. It was a picture of the Babylonians' coming along ruthlessly, without anyone to stop them, and catching people and making life cheap. Nobody worries about the life of a fish. I'm sure we are concerned about endangered species, but one individual fish or a group of fish—nobody worries about that.

Habakkuk was saying, "O Lord, is life that cheap? Are people that cheap to You that You would allow the Babylonian nation to swoop down like a group of fishermen and catch them in their nets?" This shows the helplessness of the people.

The sad thing is that the people *already* were caught in the nets of idolatry, immorality and indecency. The people of Judah were not living as they should have. God was saying, "They've already been hooked. They've already been trapped. All I'm doing is allowing them to reap exactly what they have sown."

The Haughtiness of the Enemy

Habakkuk's third argument is presented in Habakkuk 1:16,17—*the haughtiness of the enemy*. He was saying to God, "O Lord, You are promoting the pride of Babylon." Babylon was a proud nation. They were haughty. When you see the art that they produced, when you see the buildings that they put up, you can just see that everything reeked of pride. They thought they were the greatest nation that ever appeared. "Therefore, they sacrifice unto their net, and burn incense unto their drag, because by them their portion is fat, and their food plenteous" (v. 16).

This goes back to what he said in verse 11—that they made power their god. In other words, they worshiped the god of power. They worshiped the means that permitted them to trap other people and to loot from them.

Nations today do this. People worship power. They worship the means to wealth and the means to power. They forget God. Babylon was living in luxury. Their food was plenteous, their portion was fat. "Shall they, therefore, empty their net, and not spare continually to slay the nations?" (v. 17). They caught one group of nations, they emptied the net, and then they went out and filled it up again. Wouldn't they ever be satisfied?

As a nation marches along and wins one victory after another, it becomes proud. People begin to worship their means. They begin to worship their ammunition. They begin to worship all that they have—their industry and their accomplishments. They get proud.

We have proud nations today, nations that boast of their munitions and their technology. It wouldn't take much for God to put those nations out of existence. So we see the haughtiness of the enemy. "God, how can You allow these proud people to get even prouder by swooping down upon the people of Judah?" Of course, the answer is that their pride is going to destroy them.

Pride always goes before destruction, and a haughty spirit always goes before a fall (see Prov. 16:18). We're going to discover that when we look at Habakkuk 2.

Here then are three arguments that the prophet gave to God, trying to convince God to change His mind: The holiness of God—how can a holy God permit an unholy nation to attack His own people? The helplessness of the people—they were like fish caught in a net. The haughtiness of the enemy—they were proud, worshiping their means of destruction, without mercy and without forgiveness.

Are you arguing with God? Are you trying to convince God that He should change His plans just to please you? Don't do it, because the great message of Habakkuk is this: The just shall live by faith.

The prophet was worrying and wondering. At the end of this book he's going to be worshiping and witnessing. He's going to go from the valley of despair to the mountain peaks of praise and victory. And how does he do this? *He learns to trust God.* He learns to leave it all with the Lord, who said, "Be still, and know that I am God" (Ps. 46:10). Don't argue with God. Listen to God, and trust Him, and He'll work it out in His time.

Chapter 5

Stars in the Storm

(Hab. 2:1-4,14,20)

In Habakkuk 1 the prophet had been worrying and wondering. He'd been debating with God, trying to convince God to change His mind. In chapter 2 the prophet watched and waited. "I will stand upon my watch, and set myself upon the tower, and will watch to see what he will say unto me, and what I shall answer when I am reproved" (v. 1).

Habakkuk gave God a chance to answer him. So often in the problems of life we do so much talking that we don't take time to listen. I've noticed in my pastoral ministry that this is often the case with people who have problems. They'll come in and talk and talk and ask you for advice and ask you for counsel, but you don't have a chance to say anything to them. They always feel better after they have unloaded their feelings on you, so perhaps you do some good after all.

God did answer the Prophet Habakkuk. God answered by giving him a vision of what the world is like and what God is doing. "And the Lord answered me, and said, Write the vision, and make it plain upon tablets, that he may run that readeth it" (v. 2).

Habakkuk had a special place where he met with God. I hope you have some place where you and God can get alone with each other and where you can talk to God and God can talk to you. I know that we can talk with God and walk with God anywhere. I've had sweet fellowship with the Lord in an intensive care ward of the hospital, hovering between life and death. I have chatted with God as I have been high above the clouds in an airplane, flying above the ocean. But it's good to have one place where you can meet with God—somewhere in your home where you can open your Bible, where you can bow before the Lord in prayer and let God talk to you.

Habakkuk's Instructions

The Prophet Habakkuk received two instructions from the Lord: *Write* and *wait*.

Write

In Habakkuk 1:2 the Lord answered: "Write this vision. I want it to be permanent. I want you to write it down because future generations are going to need it. And write it in such a way that when people read what you have to say, they can run off and share it with others." The idea is that the message was worth telling. It sounds like the Easter message, doesn't it, when the angel said, "Come and see—go and tell"? (see Matt. 28:6,7). So Habakkuk was commanded to write a clear, permanent record of what the Lord gave to him.

Wait

Second, he was commanded to *wait*. "For the vision is yet for an appointed time, but at the end it shall speak, and not lie" (Hab. 2:3). In other words, God's prophecies were going to be fulfilled. And "though it tarry, wait for it, because it will surely come, it will not tarry" (v. 3). Our problem, of course, is that we get so nervous and so anxious that we cannot wait on God.

This promise is quoted in Hebrews 10:35-38: "Cast not away, therefore, your confidence, which hath great recompense of reward. For ye have need of patience that, after ye have done the will of God, ye might receive the promise. For yet a little while, and he that shall come will come, and will not tarry. Now the just shall live by faith."

You can see the connection between Hebrews 10 and Habakkuk 2. In Hebrews 10 the little word "it" becomes "he." "For yet a little while, and he that shall come will come, and will not tarry." The Holy Spirit applies this to the Lord Jesus Christ. We are waiting for the Lord Jesus to return. And when He returns, He will judge sin, and He will establish His glorious reign.

God's Condemnation of Babylon

The prophet was commanded to write, and he was commanded to wait. Then God gave to him the vision. As you read Habakkuk 2, you'll notice that there is a dark background of judgment, the wrath of God. Five woes are listed in chapter 2: "Woe to him that increaseth that which is not his!" (v. 6). This is a woe, a condemnation, against selfish ambition. "Woe to him that coveteth" (v. 9). This is a condemnation of covetousness. "Woe to him that buildeth a town with blood" (v. 12). God condemned exploiting the people. "Woe unto him that giveth his neighbor drink" (v. 15)—a condemnation of strong drink and drunkenness. "Woe unto him that saith to the wood, Awake; to the dumb stone, Arise, it shall teach!" (v. 19)—a woe against idolatry.

Here we have five woes. These sins were being committed by the nation of Babylon, but they were committing these sins because of their *pride*. In verses 4 and 5, God condemned the pride of Babylon, and then He condemned their selfish ambition, their covetousness, their exploiting of people, their drunkenness and their idolatry.

But the interesting thing is this: Some of these sins were taking place in the nation of Judah. Some individuals in Judah were proud and greedy, and they were plundering. Some in Judah were adding to their real estate by exploiting the poor. Some in Judah were guilty of drunkenness and idolatry.

We want God to judge the sins of *other* nations, but we don't want God to judge *our own sins*. We read the newspapers and say, "God should do something about these things." But then we don't want Him to do anything about those same things in our own lives. How easy it is to be convicted about other people's sins!

Three Assurances

Against this dark background of judgment and wrath—the wrath of God leveled against these awful sins—we have three very wonderful assurances. They shine like stars in a storm. In Habakkuk 2:4,14,20, to encourage the prophet and to encourage you and me today, God gave us these three very wonderful assurances.

Assurance of God's Grace

First of all is *the assurance of God's grace.* "Behold, his soul that is lifted up is not upright in him; but the just shall live by his faith" (Hab. 2:4). The first half of that verse describes the Babylonians—the proud, puffed-up Babylonians. The last half of that verse is talking about the believer. "The just shall live by his faith." This is the assurance of the grace of God.

We cannot overestimate or overstate the importance of this verse. If you were to ask me what one of the most important verses in the Old Testament is, I would say Habakkuk 2:4. This verse is so important that it is quoted and explained in three books in the New Testament.

You'll find it in Romans 1:17 where the theme of the book is *the just.* How can a sinner be justified before God? This verse is quoted in Galatians 3:11 where the theme of the book is how the just *shall live.* If you want to know what it means to live by the grace of God, you should read Galatians. It's quoted in Hebrews 10:38 where the theme of the book is *by faith.* And so this little statement "The just shall live by his faith" is amplified in three books in the New Testament: Romans talks about the just, Galatians talks about how they shall live, and Hebrews explains the little phrase "by faith."

The contrast in Habakkuk 2:4 is between the pride of Babylon and the faith of the believers in Judah. Babylon was puffed up: "Behold, his soul that is lifted up" (v. 4). The Hebrew word means puffed up.

The Babylonians were self-sufficient. They were important. People who live by faith are not puffed up, because faith has a way of humbling you. When you live by faith, you are trusting God, not trusting yourself. The Babylonian's desires were not right: "Behold, his soul that is lifted up is not upright in him" (v. 4). The Babylonians didn't desire the things that were right. They were not straight; they were crooked in character. The opposite of faith is not unbelief; it is really pride. Proud people don't trust. Proud people take care of things all by themselves. Babylon didn't have to trust God. They had their munitions, they had their armies, they had everything they needed.

As you look at this dark world and realize how much sin there is in the world, just remember the assurance of God's grace: "The just shall live by his faith" (v. 4). You can make it by faith. You can't make it by yourself. If you puff yourself up and try to build yourself up to do your own thing, eventually you are going to be judged. If you trust the Lord Jesus Christ, if you yield to the Lord and let Him work things out, then you are going to be successful. We have in Habakkuk 2:4 the assurance of God's grace: "The just shall live by his faith."

Assurance of God's Glory

In Habakkuk 2:14 we have *the assurance of God's glory*: "For the earth shall be filled with the knowledge of the glory of the Lord, as the waters cover the sea."

What is the glory of the Lord? The glory of the Lord means the sum of all of God's attributes. Glory is not just an attribute of God; glory is the characteristic of all His attributes. He is glorious in wisdom, glorious in power, glorious in grace, glorious in mercy. God's glory means all that He is and all that He does, and He is unique. There is no one who has glory as God has glory.

The statement that the earth "shall be filled with the knowledge of the glory of the Lord, as the waters cover the sea" is not a new statement. Back in Numbers 14, when the people of Israel disobeyed at Kadesh-Barnea and would not go into the Promised Land, God had to judge them. Moses had to intercede for them because God threatened to destroy them. Moses prayed in Numbers 14 that God would pardon their sin: "And the Lord said, I have pardoned according to thy word; but as truly as I live, all the earth shall be filled with the glory of the Lord" (vv. 20,21). The nation of Israel was going to lose the glory of the Lord. They were going to wander around in the wilderness for 40 years. But God said, "One of these days the earth shall be filled with the glory of the Lord. I'm not going to allow the unbelief and the disobedience of wicked people to keep Me from revealing My glory."

In Isaiah 6, when Isaiah saw the throne room of God in heaven, he heard the seraphim calling to each other, "Holy, holy, holy, is the Lord of hosts; the whole earth is full of his glory" (v. 3). From heaven's point of view, when the angels look down on the earth, they see the glory of God. From the human point of view, I don't see much of the glory of God. I pick up the morning paper and read about murders and attacks. I read about assassinations and all kinds of wicked things, and I say, "Where is God?" But when the angels look down, they see that God is working out His plans: "The whole earth is full of his glory."

In Psalm 72:18,19 we read: "Blessed be the Lord God, the God of Israel, who only doeth wondrous things. And blessed be his glorious name forever; and let the whole earth be filled with his glory."

The promise was given to Moses: "The earth shall be filled with the glory of the Lord" (Num. 14:21). And from the perspective of heaven, the earth is filled with the glory of God. But we're also asked to pray that the earth will be filled with the glory of God: "Thy kingdom come. Thy will be done in earth, as it is in heaven" (Matt. 6:10).

This is the assurance of God's glory. It's interesting to trace the glory of God in the Old Testament. Moses dedicated the tabernacle, and God's glory moved in (see Ex. 40:34,35). Then Israel sinned against the Lord, and God wrote: "Ichabod, the glory has departed" (see I Sam. 4:21). The Israelites built the temple, and the glory of God moved in (see II Chron. 5:13,14). If you'll read the first 11 chapters of Ezekiel, you'll see the glory departing. The glory did not return to Israel until Jesus came and "we beheld his glory, the glory as of the only begotten of the Father" (John 1:14).

But the Jewish people took the Lord Jesus and crucified Him. So did the Romans. All of us were involved in the death of Jesus Christ on the cross. And the glory, as it were, was covered by the darkness of sin.

Today the glory of God dwells in His Church and in the bodies of His people, and one day that glory is going to cover the earth, "as the waters cover the sea" (Hab. 2:14).

Assurance of God's Government

In Habakkuk 2:20 you have a third wonderful assurance, *the assurance of God's government.* "But the Lord is in his holy temple; let all the earth keep silence before him." God is in control; so be submissive. Don't argue. Don't try to tell God what to do. God is in heaven. God is on the throne, and He is caring for His own. He knows what He is doing.

It must have been a great assurance to Habakkuk to realize that God was in His holy temple. The Babylonians might invade and destroy the temple on earth, but the temple in heaven was going to be kept pure and holy. No one could invade that temple.

Here we have God's government. God is in control—be submissive. God is in control—be silent. "Let all the earth keep silence before him" (v. 20).

In chapter 1 of Habakkuk the prophet did a great deal of talking. He argued with God and asked questions: "Why? How long? Why?" God said to him, "Now look, I am in My holy temple. I know what I am doing. Just keep quiet. 'Be still, and know that I am God' (Ps. 46:10)."

If you look at this world today and see only the woes, you are going to be discouraged. We look around and we see sin as did Habakkuk—selfish ambition, covetousness. We see people murdering and killing and exploiting. We see drunkenness and idolatry. But the prophet says to us, "Don't just look at the woes. Lift your eyes a little higher and see God." See the grace of God—"The just shall live by his faith" (Hab. 2:4). See the glory of God—"The earth shall be filled with the knowledge of the glory of the Lord, as the waters cover the sea" (v. 14). And see the government of God—"But the Lord is in his holy temple; let all the earth keep silence before him" (v. 20).

Which part of Habakkuk 2:4 are you living in? The first part—puffed up with pride and self-sufficiency? Then you will fall. Or are you living in the last part—"The just shall live by his faith"? If you live by faith, you will end up singing praises to God as Habakkuk did.

Chapter 6

The Peril of Pride

(Hab. 2:4-8)

Thomas Jefferson wrote in 1784: "I tremble for my country when I reflect that God is just, that His justice cannot sleep forever." The Prophet Habakkuk was trembling for his country—the nation of Judah—but he thought that God was *unjust*. God was using the wicked nation of Babylon to chasten Judah, but who was going to judge Babylon? God declared Babylon's judgment in a series of five woes given in Habakkuk 2—five woes that denounced the sins of that nation.

In verses 6-8 God denounced their selfish ambition, in verses 9-11 their covetousness, in verses 12-14 their exploitation of people. Then in verses 15-17 He pronounced woe upon those who promote strong drink and drunkenness. Finally, in verses 18-20, God denounced those who were involved in idolatry.

But the root of these five horrible sins is given in Habakkuk 2:4,5—the sin of pride. Babylon would eventually be destroyed by her own sins. The Bible says, "Be sure your sin will find you out" (Num.

32:23). That doesn't simply mean that sin will one day be exposed. It means that sin will be exposed by the judgment that it brings.

Sometimes our sins slumber, and they don't produce judgment right away. Sometimes when we sin, we immediately face the consequences of that sin. Babylon eventually was judged, and her own sins brought her downfall. You and I had better avoid these same sins. It's easy for us to look at ancient history and say, "Isn't it terrible that Babylon was so proud, selfish and covetous? How awful that Babylon exploited people and used them to foster her own purposes, that Babylon was a nation given to drinking and idolatry!" How easy it is to convict someone in ancient history. But what about nations today? Are nations today given to drinking and idolatry? Are nations today exploiting people, using them like things and, when they're through with them, tossing them away? Are they covetous? Do they have selfish ambitions? Yes, they do. Why? Because individual people are guilty of these sins. And the root of these sins is pride. Many theologians believe that pride is the essence of all sin.

Babylon would eventually be destroyed by her own sin. And if you and I practice these sins, they will destroy us.

The Sin of Pride

Let's consider the sin of pride. Speaking about the Babylonians, Habakkuk 2:4,5 says, "Behold, his soul that is lifted up is not upright in him; but the just shall live by his faith. Yea, also, because he [the wine

Babylonians] transgresseth by wine, he is a proud man, neither keepeth at home, who enlargeth his desire as sheol [hell], and is as death, and cannot be satisfied, but gathereth unto himself all nations, and heapeth unto himself all peoples."

Pride Puffs Us Up

What does pride do to us? To begin with, pride puffs us up. "Behold, his soul that is lifted up [puffed up within him] is not upright in him" (Hab. 2:4). Pride has a way of puffing us up so that we have a false estimate of ourselves. Some Christians *grow*, and some Christians just *swell*. You can always tell whether or not a person has true humility. When he has an opportunity to "shine," he prefers to let somebody else shine.

Small people, when they get proud, think they are very big. A famous Englishman once said, "When small men cast long shadows, it's a sign that the sun is setting." That's true. We have today those who, because of their pride, look big, but they aren't really big. They are just swollen. Pride has a way of puffing us up and giving us a false estimate of how big we are. When you live like this, your character is eroded. Character, not reputation, is what makes a person great—not what I think I am or what people say I am but what God knows I am. Pride has a way of puffing us up.

Pride Twists Us

Pride has a way of twisting us. "Behold, his soul that is lifted up is not upright in him" (Hab. 2:4).

That phrase means that he is twisted; he is not straight. Pride has a way of setting its own standards. "Well, everybody does it; why shouldn't I? I'm as important as he is. Why, if she can do it, so can I." Pride has a way of saying, "I'm going to do it *my way*. I'm going to get what *I* want, and I don't care who is hurt by it." Pride has a way of twisting our character and making us crooked.

Pride Makes Us Restless

Pride has a way of making us restless. Notice what Habakkuk 2:5 says: "He transgresseth by wine, he is a proud man, neither keepeth at home." Literally, it means he is never at rest because he's drunk with pride. That's quite an image, isn't it? He compares the proud man to the drunken man. A drunken man thinks he is strong; he can fight anybody, because he really doesn't have control of his thinking. A drunken man will have a false joy, a false sense of achievement. A drunken man feels he can do anything, that he is really big. So it is with pride. A person drunk with pride, however, is restless. *There is no peace in pride.* Do you know why? Pride brings competition. If I start measuring myself and seeing how big I am, then I must start measuring other people to see whether or not they are bigger than I am. This is one of the problems the disciples had. They were forever arguing over who was the greatest. Jesus said, "You're measuring yourself by the wrong standard. Put yourself next to a child" (see Luke 9:46-48). "But a child is much smaller than I am." But the child is greater because the child is humble, the child knows it is a child, and the child is not seeking for false greatness.

What does pride do to us? It puffs us up so we think we are bigger than we really are. It twists us so that our character is eroded. It makes us restless. There is no peace for those who are proud. They're always afraid of being knocked off of their throne. They're always afraid somebody's going to come along with a needle and puncture them and deflate them.

Pride Makes Us Greedy

Pride does something else to us: It makes us greedy. Habakkuk 2:5 says, "Who enlargeth his desire as sheol [hell, or the grave]." Death is very greedy. We talk about people who are as greedy as death. Death is always out to claim someone. The grave is always looking for someone. The proud person gets greedy. He's always wanting to get more and more. The Babylonians were this way. They weren't satisfied with their great empire in Babylon; they had to swoop down and take over one nation after another. Did they need those nations? No. Did they want those nations? Yes. Why did they want them? They were proud. They were restless. They weren't satisfied with what they had. Like a drunken person, they were greedy for more.

First the man takes the drink, then the drink takes the drink, and then the drink takes the man. Babylon got drunk with pride, and pride has to be fed constantly, just as a drunken man has to keep on drinking.

God had something to say about Babylon's pride. Keep in mind that Jeremiah and Habakkuk were contemporaries ministering in the city of Jerusalem. Jeremiah 50:31,32 says, "Behold, I am against thee, O thou most proud, saith the Lord God of hosts; for thy day is come, the time that I will punish thee. And the most proud shall stumble and fall, and none shall raise him up; and I will kindle a fire in his cities, and it shall devour all round about him." He was talking about the judgment of Babylon.

"Pride goeth before destruction, and an haughty spirit before a fall" (Prov. 16:18). Babylon was headed for a big fall!

The nations that had been conquered by Babylon took up a taunting song against Babylon. "Shall not all these [defeated nations] take up a parable against him, and a taunting proverb against him" (Hab. 2:6). Habakkuk pictured the nations' getting together as a choir, and instead of saying, "Woe is us," they are saying, "Woe unto Babylon!" Instead of saying, "Woe, what has God done to us!" they're saying, "Woe, what God is going to do to Babylon!"

Woe Upon Selfish Ambition

In Habakkuk 2:6-8 we have the first of these five woes—judgment against their selfish ambition: "Woe to him that increaseth that which is not his! How long? And to him that ladeth himself with thick clay! Shall they not rise up suddenly that shall bite thee, and awake that shall vex thee, and thou shalt be for booty unto them? Because thou hast spoiled many nations, all the remnant of the peoples shall spoil thee, because of men's blood, and for the violence of the land, of the city, and of all that dwell therein."

There's nothing wrong with *godly* ambition. In II Corinthians 5:9 Paul wrote: "Wherefore, we labor that, whether present or absent, we may be accepted of him." That phrase "we labor" means "we are ambitious." It's a good thing to be ambitious to please the Lord.

Paul used the same word in Romans 15:20: "Yea, so have I strived to preach the gospel, not where Christ was named." That word "strived" is "I was ambitious." "So have I been ambitious to preach the Gospel where Christ has never been preached." There's nothing wrong with *godly* ambition. If a man has a godly desire to see his Sunday school increase—not pride but a godly desire—this is a good thing. We ought to have godly desires to "grow in grace, and in the knowledge of our Lord and Savior, Jesus Christ" (II Pet. 3:18). There ought to be a godly ambition in our lives to better understand the Word of God and to be better witnesses for the Lord Jesus. There is nothing wrong with godly ambition. But the thing God condemns is *selfish* ambition, success at any price.

Robbers and Debtors

God described these people, first of all, as *robbers*. They were piling up loot that didn't belong to them. They were stealing. "Woe to him that increaseth that which is not his!" (Hab. 2:6). So they were robbers. And yet He said they were *debtors.* The little phrase "and to him that ladeth himself with thick clay" (v. 6) is difficult for us to understand. They used to give clay tablets as a pledge, or a receipt, when someone borrowed money or merchandise. What God was saying is this: When the Babylonians swooped down on other nations and stole all of the wealth, they were really only *borrowing* it. They were heaping up a lot of debt, and payday was going to come someday.

It looked as if Babylon was getting away with everything. But they weren't getting away with anything at all. Whenever we sin and rob somebody else, we are adding up for ourselves a debt that is going to be paid with compound interest. We are debtors. The Babylonians were collecting receipts for loans, and God, through the prophet, said, "One of these days your creditors are going to exact justice on you. 'Be sure your sin will find you out' (Num. 32:23)." If we sow to the flesh, we will of the flesh reap corruption (see Gal. 6:8). A person will reap exactly what he sows. "Be not deceived, God is not mocked, for whatever a man soweth, that shall he also reap" (v. 7). These nations were going to exact the debt one of these days, and judgment was going to come.

Losers

These people were also called *losers.* "Because thou hast spoiled many nations, all the remnant of the peoples shall spoil thee" (Hab. 2:8). You're going to get what you give. You're going to reap what you've sown. There is a law of compensation in this world that says you don't get away with anything. It may look like you're getting away with it, but you aren't. True success is not spoiling other people; true success is not robbing from others; true success is not born of pride. True success is humility in service. The Babylonians were proud. Jesus said that if you want to be a true success, you must be humble. The Babylonians had selfish ambition. They were grasping what didn't belong to them. Jesus said that if you want to be a success, don't grasp—give. Don't take away from others, but share what you have.

I fear that today we have in our society a false view of success. We have a worldly attitude toward success. Success to us means that you are big—you are important and puffed up. Jesus said, "No, success means that you make other people important. Other people will be more important to you than you are to yourself. You will love your neighbor as yourself, and you will treat your neighbor as God has treated you." True success does not mean selfish ambition, it means being ambitious to please the Lord and to serve others.

What is your view of success? As you measure your life and your ministry, what is your view of success? You and I may be guilty of some of these sins. Pride and selfish ambition may be lurking in our hearts. And God warns us: "These sins will find you out and cause you to stumble."

Allow me to remind you once again that humility—not pride—and willing service—not selfish ambition—are the marks of true success because this is the way Jesus lived. He told His disciples, "I am among you as One who serves" (see Luke 22:27).

Chapter 7

The Curse of Covetousness

(Hab. 2:9-14)

As the Prophet Habakkuk stood on his watchtower, he saw the hordes of Babylonian soldiers, like hungry animals, sweeping down upon the helpless people of Judah. Would anything stop them? Would their sins ever be judged? Yes, they would be judged. God would one day judge Babylon for her sins, just as one day He will judge all people and all nations that rebel against Him.

In Habakkuk 2:4,5 we looked at the basis, the fundamental cause, of their sin—their pride. They were puffed up with pride. They had gone from victory to victory. They were the great nation of Babylon! Their pride led to selfish ambition (vv. 6-8). That is the first of five woes in Habakkuk 2. God pronounced woe upon them because of their selfish ambition, for taking that which did not belong to them and using it for their own selfish purposes.

In verses 9-11 He pronounced woe upon their *covetousness,* and then in verses 12-14 He pronounced woe upon their *exploitation of people.*

Woe Upon Covetousness

"Woe to him that coveteth an evil covetousness to his house, that he may set his nest on high, that he may be delivered from the power of evil! Thou hast plotted shame to thy house by cutting off many peoples, and hast sinned against thy soul. For the stone shall cry out of the wall, and the beam out of the timber shall answer it" (Hab. 2:9-11).

What is covetousness? Covetousness is the desire for more. Covetousness is that appetite of the soul that says, "I cannot be satisfied unless I get more." "Thou shalt not covet" is the last of the Ten Commandments (Ex. 20:17). And yet covetousness would cause a person to disobey *all* of the commandments. Because people are covetous, they will be idolators. Because people are covetous, they will blaspheme the name of God. Covetousness would make a person murder or steal or dishonor his father and mother. Covetousness would cause a person to commit adultery. The covetous heart and the proud heart, together, lead people into sin.

Building an Estate

The picture here is of a very successful man building his estate. He covets more land and more houses. The word "house" in verses 9 and 10 may refer to the physical structure. It also may refer to the family, because in the Old Testament a man was building his house when he was adding to his family. Both of these are true. The Babylonians were great builders. They built Babylon. "Is not this great

Babylon, that I have built?" asked King Nebuchadnezzar (Dan. 4:30).

The man in Habakkuk 2:9,10 is building his house. He's building a physical structure, and he's building his family. The Babylonians were going to be the greatest nation on the face of the earth. What did they do? They got their real estate by stealing it from others, by force and by murder. Babylon was taking land that did not belong to her.

In verse 8 we discover that the Babylonians were taking land by blood and by violence. They were capturing cities and forcing the people in the cities to become their slaves.

So this is a picture of a man building his estate. He wants to add more property. He wants to add more buildings. He wants more room for his family. And his goal is security. That's a popular word today, isn't it? Security. People want security. They want to know that their money is secure in the bank. They go to the doctor to make sure their health is somewhat secure. They take their car to the mechanic to be sure that when they leave on vacation, everything is secure in the mechanics of the car. People want security.

Building a Nest on High

Babylon wanted to "set his nest on high, that he may be delivered from the power of evil!" (Hab. 2:9). This continues the image that was used back in chapter 1, where God pictured the Babylonians as fierce animals, swooping down upon the nation of Judah. "Their horses also are swifter than the leopards, and are more fierce than the evening wolves; and their horsemen shall spread themselves, and their horsemen shall come from far; they shall fly like the eagle that hasteth to eat" (v. 8).

Daniel pictured the Babylonian empire as a lion with wings. The Babylonian said, "I'm going to set my nest on high. I'm going to be like the eagle. I'm going to get where nobody can touch me. I am going to be safe and secure."

I suppose an eagle's nest would be among the most secure in all of nature. The eagle goes high in the mountains and builds and protects her nest. But this is a false security. When you disobey God and rebel against His Word, there is no place where you can hide.

Obadiah 1:4 says, "Though thou exalt thyself like the eagle, and though thou set thy nest among the stars, from there will I bring thee down, saith the Lord." So Babylon sat very secure, but then along came the Medes and the Persians and defeated them. In one night everything changed.

There is no security outside the will of God. A covetous person says, "I'm going to get more! If I have more land, more houses, more workers and more money, I will be secure." Actually, there is no security in covetousness because the covetous person always needs a little bit more. His problem is not security, his problem is selfishness. Covetousness is born of pride and insecurity. That's why God said in Habakkuk 2:10, "Thou hast plotted shame to thy house by cutting off many peoples, and hast sinned against thy soul." In other words, he was trying to build his house to show off. He was going to have security; he was going to have something to brag about. But God said, "No, the way you've done it you ought to be ashamed of what you did. You've built your house with blood. You have hurt other people. You have sinned against your own soul."

This is why the Lord Jesus said in Luke 12:15, "Take heed, and beware of covetousness; for a man's life consisteth not in the abundance of the things which he possesseth." He gave the parable about the farmer who had a bumper crop and didn't know what to do. He said, "What am I going to do with all that I have?" (see v. 17).

When you're covetous, you think that you can do whatever you want to with your possessions. I would remind you that you and I don't own anything. We are stewards of what God has given to us.

"And he [the farmer] said, This will I do: I will pull down my barns, and build greater; and there will I bestow all my crops and my goods. And I will say to my soul, Soul, thou hast much goods laid up for many years; take thine ease. Eat, drink, and be merry" (vv. 18,19). This was false security.

If you have some extra money in the bank, if you receive a promotion at work, it may lead you to have a sense of false security. As God said to the farmer, "Thou fool, this night thy soul shall be required of thee" (v. 20).

There is nothing wrong with saving. There is nothing wrong with having something set aside for the future. The Bible doesn't teach that we should be careless with what God has given to us. But the Bible does warn us against covetousness: "Take heed, and beware of covetousness" (v. 15). Why? What's so dangerous about covetousness? Well, it makes us treat people like things. Covetousness gives us a false sense of security. We begin to think that we don't need God anymore. Covetousness never satisfies us. We sin against our own soul, and one day that which we have taken wrongly will testify against us.

Habakkuk 2:11 says, "For the stone shall cry out of the wall, and the beam out of the timber shall answer it." This is a remarkable statement. God says that the very house you build will witness against you. You may finish building the house and move in and say, "Now, I have arrived," but every timber in that house cost somebody his blood. Every stone in that house cost somebody hard work and labor. And every time you are in that house, it is going to witness against you because you have sinned against the Lord.

James 5:1-4 states the same idea: "Come now, ye rich men, weep and howl for your miseries that shall come upon you. Your riches are corrupted and your garments are motheaten. Your gold and silver are rusted, and the rust of them shall be a witness against you, and shall eat your flesh as it were fire. Ye have heaped treasure together for the last days. Behold, the hire of the laborers who have reaped down your fields, which is of you kept back by fraud, crieth." In other words, the money the employers should have given in wages they kept.

But that very money witnesses against them. All the gold and silver they have collected witnesses against them, and they cannot enjoy it. Covetousness is a terrible sin.

Woe Upon Exploitation

Habakkuk 2:12-14 deals with another sin: *exploitation of the people.* "Woe to him that buildeth a town with blood [bloodshed], and establisheth a city by iniquity [crime]!" The sin here is forced labor. The Babylonians would capture people and make slaves out of them. The Egyptians did the same thing with the Jews. You have no idea how much blood went into the building of those great projects of Babylon! "Behold, is it not of the Lord of hosts that the peoples shall labor only for fire, and the nations shall weary themselves for nothing?" (v. 13). You exploit somebody when you take more than you give, when you treat people like things. You exploit people when they have to work harder for you than you would work for them. You exploit people when you make them do things you wouldn't do yourself. A great deal of exploiting is going on today.

Babylon had great building projects, but they were built on bloodshed. To them *things* were more important than *people*. God, through Habakkuk, said, "All right, go ahead and build these things. You're building a town with blood; you're establishing a city by crime and forced labor and slavery, but it's not of the Lord. God didn't do it, and therefore, it's not going to last. The people shall labor only for fire." That's an interesting statement. What's going to happen to all of these things? They'll be burned up.

We see this happening today. Some people are exploiting the poor. Some are exploiting God's people. There are nations in this world where there is slave labor, where human rights are being violated. Many people are being exploited so that a few people might be able to get what they want. And God says, "I'm not doing that. This is not My work; this is your work, and it's all going to be burned up. You are wearing yourself out for nothing." Imagine that! All of this toil, all of this exploiting, all of this work, and where will it end? Nowhere; it is all vanity.

But verse 14 is the answer to all of this: "For the earth shall be filled with the knowledge of the glory of the Lord, as the waters cover the sea." We don't see much of the glory of the Lord today, do we? We look around, and we see covetousness, pride and exploiting going on. But God says that one day there will be glory.

In Numbers 14:21 God said, "As truly as I live, all the earth shall be filled with the glory of the Lord." In Isaiah 6:3 one of the seraphim called to the other and said, "Holy, holy, holy, is the Lord of hosts; the whole earth is full of his glory."

We pray according to Psalm 72:19, "And blessed be his glorious name forever; and let the whole earth be filled with his glory."

Whatever you do for the glory of God is going to last. Whatever you do in obedience to the will of God is going to last. Human plans for utopia are all going to fail. People are not going to fill the earth with their glory. God is going to fill the earth with His glory. Mankind has always wanted to build a utopia. Man has shed blood, murdered, lied and created war. And yet we do not see much glory in the world today. Do you know why? All the glory of flesh is like the glory of the grass (see I Pet. 1:24). It doesn't last. Man's glory is so temporary. But God's glory is eternal. The promise is given to us that "the earth shall be filled with the knowledge of the glory of the Lord, as the waters cover the sea" (Hab. 2:14). This will happen when our Lord Jesus comes, when sin is judged, when justice is established and when glory emanates from His throne.

May the Lord help us not to get involved in the sins of covetousness and exploiting other people. May the Lord give us instead hearts that share, hearts that give, hearts that serve, hearts that love our neighbors. May the Lord help us to be part of the answer and not part of the problem.

Chapter 8

The Dangers of Drink

(Hab. 2:15-17)

The nation of Babylon was noted for its devotion to wine and strong drink. In fact, God pictured Babylon's conquest by using the image of a cup of wine. "Babylon hath been a golden cup in the Lord's hand, that made all the earth drunk; the nations have drunk of her wine; therefore, the nations are mad" (Jer. 51:7).

The image of a cup of wine was not an unusual one in that day. The Lord pictured Babylon as a drunken nation that was overflowing the other nations, and yet her judgment was going to come. He said that He was going to send judgment upon Babylon: "I will make drunk her princes, and her wise men" (v. 57). In other words, the nation that was trying to make others drunk was herself going to fall in her own drunken stupor.

Woe Upon Those Given to Strong Drink

This brings us to Habakkuk 2:15-17, the fourth of the woes that God pronounced upon the nation of Babylon. It was the woe to those who are given to strong drink. "Woe unto him that giveth his neighbor drink, that puttest thy wineskin to him, and makest him drunk also, that thou mayest look on their nakedness! Thou art filled with shame for glory; drink thou also, and let thy shame come upon thee; the cup of the Lord's right hand shall be turned unto thee, and shameful spewing shall be on thy glory. For the violence of Lebanon shall cover thee, and the spoil of beasts, which made them afraid, because of men's blood, and for the violence of the land, of the city, and of all that dwell therein."

This is not a very beautiful picture, is it? What he's saying is that the nation of Babylon is going to be condemned because of their addiction to strong drink.

I think that we need to deal with this in some detail because alcohol consumption is America's number one drug problem. When you read in the newspapers about the people who are being picked up for using cocaine or marijuana or some other narcotic, just remember, the number one drug problem in the United States of America is alcohol. Eleven to 17 million Americans are considered to be alcoholic. Americans spend about $50 billion a year on alcohol. People complain because of the amount of money that's spent on missiles or other things, and yet Americans spend $50 billion a year on alcohol! You may say, "Well, people make money from the sale of alcohol."

Alcohol *problems* cost the American economy an estimated $68.6 billion each year. These are problems that result from people who drink—

physical problems, jobs that are lost, man-hours that are lost on the job, accidents on the highway. Did you know that the leading cause of mental retardation is alcohol consumption during pregnancy? More than 250,000 Americans lost their lives in alcohol-related accidents during the past ten years—that's 25,000 a year! One person dies every 21 minutes in an alcohol-related auto wreck. That's about 70 a day. On an average weekend night, one out of every ten drivers on the road is drunk.

Alcohol consumption is the leading cause of death for persons between the ages of 15 and 24—not *elderly* people but young people between the ages of 15 and 24. Eighty-three percent of all fire fatalities are alcohol related. Fifty to 68 percent of all drownings are alcohol related. Up to 80 percent of all suicides are related to alcohol, and up to 40 percent of all fatal industrial accidents are connected with alcohol. Eighty-six percent of all murders are alcohol related.

I see a great deal in the newspapers about child abuse. Sixty-five percent of the child abuse cases are connected with alcohol. And at least 200,000 Americans die *each year* either because of their own or somebody else's alcohol consumption.

These statistics come from the *Third and Fourth Special Reports to the U.S. Congress on Alcohol and Health.* They are not very beautiful statistics.

Sins That Alcohol Breeds

Consider the terrible sins that alcohol breeds in the lives of individuals and nations. Someone has said that in Washington, D.C., we have three parties: the Republican Party, the Democratic Party and the cocktail party. The amount of alcohol consumed on government premises and for government purposes in Washington, D.C., is appalling.

Immorality

In Habakkuk 2:15 we have the first sin that comes from alcohol, and that's *immorality*. The verse speaks about a man who gets his neighbor drunk so that he might look upon his nakedness. Drinking and immorality go together. When people start drinking, they start lowering their standards; they start losing their control. The Bible says we should love our neighbor as ourself (see Mark 12:31). Habakkuk 2:15 says, "Woe unto him that giveth his neighbor drink." Today it seems that the most social thing you can do is to give your neighbor a drink. The first question I'm asked in a restaurant is "Would you like to have a cocktail?" When you get on an airplane, before you know it, they turn the airplane into a cocktail lounge. And these lovely girls who are supposed to be stewardesses become barmaids! They ask you, "What would you like to drink?" My Bible says, "Woe unto him that giveth his neighbor drink." The motive behind offering the drink is immorality. The motive of the stewardess or the waitress is certainly not that. But I think there's a principle involved here.

This verse reminds me of what happened to Noah. He got drunk (see Gen. 9:20-23), and he was uncovered within his tent, because drunkenness and immorality always go together. Ham, the father of Canaan, saw the nakedness of his father and told his two brothers about it. He joked about it. But Shem and Japheth did the loving thing. God's Word says that love covers a multitude of sins (see I Pet. 4:8). They put a garment over their shoulders and walked backward so that they wouldn't see their father's nakedness, and they covered him.

Noah was a good man, a godly man, one of God's great servants. He got drunk, and he got involved in immorality. Drink leads to immodest behavior, immorality.

Shame

Drinking also leads to *shame*. Habakkuk 2:16 says, "Thou art filled with shame for glory." In other words, those who drink like to glory in what they're doing. It never ceases to amaze me how people brag about their sins. Philippians 3:19 talks about people who glory in their shame. They brag about the things they ought to be ashamed of. You hear people at work bragging about how drunk they were over the weekend, bragging about some drunken party somewhere. I wouldn't brag about that. I'd be ashamed of it. "Thou art filled with shame for glory." What our Lord was saying here is simply this: "Today, in your drunken stupor, you're boasting and bragging, but one of these days all of the glory you think you have is going to turn into shame. 'Drink thou also, and let thy shame come upon thee' (Hab. 2:16)."

Humanity has no permanent glory of its own.

There's nothing that man can glory in or brag about. "For all flesh is like grass, and all the glory of man like the flower of grass. The grass withereth, and its flower falleth away, but the word of the Lord endureth forever" (I Pet. 1:24,25). Man has very little glory, and when he adds alcohol to the little bit of glory he does have, he just turns that glory into shame. Oh, the people who have been disgraced because of alcohol! The nations that have been disgraced because of alcohol consumption!

Sickness

The third result that comes from alcohol is tragic, and it is *sickness*. "The cup of the Lord's right hand shall be turned unto thee, and shameful spewing shall be on thy glory" (Hab. 2:16). That's a rather delicate way of saying they're going to start vomiting. Not only are they going to throw up, but they're going to be throwing up *on their glory*. In other words, that which should have glorified God and glorified them turns out to be shame. Their glory is disgrace.

The physical results of alcohol are not unknown. People know what happens. Thomas Edison, the great inventor, said this: "To put alcohol in the body is like putting sand on the bearings of an engine. It just doesn't belong. I have a better use for my brain than to poison it with alcohol."

Doctors have stated that every drink of alcohol shortens a person's life by 20 minutes. If you want to give away your body and your life, you can do it with alcohol.

Connie Mack, who was well known in baseball for so many years, said, "I won't bother with youngsters who drink. The game requires quick thinking and clean living." And yet who sponsors athletics on television? The people who produce alcoholic beverages!

Waste

Sickness and physical consequences come from alcohol, and so does *waste*: "For the violence of Lebanon shall cover thee, and the spoil of beasts, which made them afraid, because of men's blood, and for the violence of the land, of the city, and of all that dwell therein" (Hab. 2:17). In this verse God was referring to the terrible ravages of the Babylonians against nature—against the fields and the trees and the animals. They wasted natural resources.

When the Babylonians swooped down upon a nation, they didn't let anything stand in their way. They wanted to leave behind absolute carnage and wreckage, and they did. They stripped Lebanon of the trees. The Bible often talks about the beautiful cedars of Lebanon. They stripped Lebanon of the forest.

They also participated in the mindless slaughter of beasts. There are times when animals have to be killed. Nobody argues that point. But the mindless slaughter of animals is something else.

We have this going on today. We have endangered species. For many years I've been a great admirer of whales. I think God did a magnificent piece of work when He created whales. I would love someday to go out and watch the whales. You can get on a boat and go out there among them. They're very gentle and interesting creatures. Have you ever heard the whales sing? It's an amazing thing. And yet what are nations doing today? Slaughtering them. I'm glad that the United States of America has led in the fight against the useless slaughter of whales. But we have seals and other species that are endangered. Why? Because people simply want to do their own thing. They want the resources, and this often creates new problems for us.

The Babylonians slaughtered the animals, and they ravaged the forest, and they killed the people. They weren't satisfied to come in and say, "All right, we're taking over." What did they do? They killed people uselessly.

Murders, as a result of alcohol, are common events. It's interesting that 86 percent of all murders are connected in some way with alcohol. For instance, people are having a card party, and they're drinking. Somebody has a gun, and there's an argument, and before you know it somebody's dead. Are they sorry for it? Oh, I suppose they are. But first the man takes a drink, and then the drink takes a drink, and then the drink takes the man. That's the sequence, isn't it? First the man takes the drink, and then the drink takes a drink, and then he can't stop. Then the drink takes the man, and the man murders somebody.

I know some people tell us that alcoholism is a disease. In one sense, perhaps it is. But if it is, it's the only disease we advertise, and it's the only disease we promote. Consider the waste of nature, the waste of the environment, the waste of the wonderful resources that God has given to us that results from alcohol. The cities have been ruined. It's impossible to walk through the streets of a city at night, in fact, even during the day. A drunken driver nearly killed me some years ago. A drunken driver almost killed my father. It's amazing how many people are maimed and injured for life because of someone's drunken driving.

God's wrath came down upon the nation of Babylon because of their addiction to alcohol. He made them drink the cup of wrath, and He turned their glory into shame.

I suppose this sounds like an old-fashioned sawdust trail revival message, but I think it's important for us to get concerned about these things. Sometimes we need to stand up and be counted. I do not make these things a test of fellowship, but I don't want anyone working on my staff who uses alcohol. I certainly wouldn't want any leader in a church I pastored to be even a social drinker. Paul said, "I'm not going to eat or drink; I'll not do any of these things if I make my brother stumble" (see I Cor. 8:13). I've appreciated the fact that the churches I have pastored have had a standard on alcohol. I know we can't go around looking into people's refrigerators, and we can't check their cupboards; but we can expect people to live clean lives. I've seen people converted from drunkenness and addiction to alcohol. The first thing they do is get rid of that bottle. Then they meet some Christian who says, "Oh, there's nothing wrong with it," and they're back in trouble again.

Let's keep the standards high. Let's keep our lives pure. Let's remember that God says in Habakkuk 2:15, "Woe unto him that giveth his neighbor drink." May the Lord help us to use the resources He has given us, not to create problems but to solve problems to the glory of God.

Chapter 9

The Ignorance of Idolatry

(Hab. 2:18-20)

God had one more woe to pronounce on the people of Babylon. He had pronounced four woes already—against their selfish ambition, against their covetousness, against the way they exploited people, against their addiction to strong drink. In Habakkuk 2:18-20 God pronounced judgment on the great sin of idolatry. If you'll study the archaeological records, you'll discover that Babylon was addicted to idolatry. They worshiped many gods, and they thought these gods had given them their victories.

"What profiteth the carved image that its maker hath engraved it; the melted image, and a teacher of lies, that the maker of his work trusteth in it, to make dumb idols? Woe unto him that saith to the wood, Awake; to the dumb stone, Arise, it shall teach! Behold, it is laid over with gold and silver, and there is no breath at all within it. But the Lord is in his holy temple; let all the earth keep silence before him."

What Is Idolatry?

Let's answer some important questions about the sin of idolatry. First of all, what is idolatry? The definition is given to us in Romans 1:25: "Who exchanged the truth of God for a lie, and worshiped and served the creature more than the Creator, who is blessed forever. Amen."

What is idolatry? It is worshiping and serving the creature rather than the Creator. This is what Lucifer did. When Lucifer was the exalted angel in heaven before his fall, he wanted to be God. Isaiah 14:12-14 says, "How art thou fallen from heaven, O Lucifer, son of the morning! How art thou cut down to the ground, who didst weaken the nations! For thou hast said in thine heart, I will ascend into heaven, I will exalt my throne above the stars of God; I will sit also upon the mount of the congregation, in the sides of the north, I will ascend above the heights of the clouds, I will be like the Most High." That was the satanic attack against the throne of God. And he said, "I will, I will, I will, I will, I will." He was putting *his* will against *God's* will. But God said, "No, you won't," and He cast him down. Lucifer, the son of the morning, became the prince of darkness—Satan.

It started with Satan. Idolatry means that you worship and serve the creature rather than the Creator. This was the temptation that Satan gave to Eve in the garden. " 'Ye shall be as God.' You will be your own god, and you can worship and serve the creature and not the Creator" (see Gen. 3:5).

When you know the true and the living God, you don't want substitutes. An idol is a substitute. Idolatry is ignorance. It never ceases to amaze me how classical scholars admire the culture and the religion of some of these ancient peoples. In Acts 17:30 the Apostle Paul took all of Greek history, with all of its philosophy and its idolatry, and he said, "The times of this ignorance God overlooked." Concerning all of the history that people admire, from a spiritual point of view, God said, "It's nothing but ignorance." And this is true today. Idolatry is a sin of the flesh (Gal. 5:19,20). The flesh loves idolatry because when you worship and serve the creature, you are worshiping and serving yourself.

Today we have the philosophy that says, "You just take care of number one, take care of yourself, don't worry about anybody else. If you have to walk on somebody's face to get where you want to get, you do it, because you are the important one." "Glory to man in the highest"—that is the theme song of idolatry.

What Does Idolatry Do to Us?

What does idolatry do to us? In Habakkuk 2 God, through Habakkuk, pictured a man who is making some idols. He makes the image. "What profiteth the carved image that its maker hath engraved it; the melted image" (v. 18). Three kinds of idols are mentioned: the carved image, which would be wood; the engraved image, which could be wood but was probably stone; and the molten image, which was metal. Sometimes they combined these.

Sometimes they would make a wooden image or a stone image and then cover it with gold and silver to emboss it and embellish it (v. 19). You don't want to manufacture a god that looks cheap!

The person makes the image. Isn't that interesting? You and I were made by the living God. We are made in the image of God. Idolatry means worshiping and serving the creature rather than the Creator. It means making a god after our own image. The person makes the god. Then what does he do? *He trusts the god.* He makes "the melted image, and a teacher of lies, that the maker of his work trusteth in it" (v. 18).

In verse 4 God said to Habakkuk, "The just shall live by his faith." Faith in what? Faith in the living God. But here's a man who makes a god, and then he trusts it. This god is dumb and this god is dead. It cannot speak; it cannot think; it cannot do anything. The man says, "Awake" when he speaks to the wood, and he says to the stone, "Arise." What happens? The wood doesn't wake up, and the stone doesn't arise.

It's all so very foolish. The man *makes* the image, then he *trusts* the image, and yet he knows the image doesn't have any sense. It doesn't have any life. And then the sad thing is that *he becomes like the image*—dumb and dead.

A striking passage in Psalm 115 deals with the folly of idolatry: "Not unto us, O Lord, not unto us, but unto thy name give glory, for thy mercy, and for thy truth's sake. Wherefore should the nations say, Where is now their God?" (vv. 1,2). I can just imagine somebody from Babylon or Egypt or another pagan country visiting Jerusalem and walking around and saying, "Now, where is your God? I don't see any of your gods." As you walked around the streets of Athens, there was a god on every corner. Someone jestingly said, back in the days of the great Greek empire, that there were more gods in the city of Athens than there were people. They had a god for everything. So they're walking around the city of Jerusalem saying, "Now, where is your God?" "Our God is in the heavens; he hath done whatsoever he hath pleased" (v. 3). In other words, no one made Him; He's doing what He pleases. "Their idols are silver and gold, the work of men's hands" (v. 4).

The ridicule of idolatry is mentioned in Psalm 115:5: "They have mouths, but they speak not." Imagine a god who cannot talk to you. "Eyes have they, but they see not" (v. 5). Such a god cannot even see you or recognize you. "They have ears, but they hear not" (v. 6). You can't pray to them. "Noses have they, but they smell not" (v. 6). You can't offer them sacrifices; they don't even know you're doing it. "They have hands, but they handle not" (v. 7). They can't help you in any way. If you're in trouble, their hands aren't going to move. "Feet have they, but they walk not" (v. 7). They aren't going to go with you. They can't be in your presence when you're having difficulties or problems. "Neither speak they through their throat" (v. 7). Not only do they not speak, they can't even make any kind of noise. These are the dumb, dead idols. "They who make them are like unto them" (v. 8). That is a devastating statement. "So is every one who trusteth in them" (v. 8). *You become like the god that you worship.* If you worship a dead god, you're dead. If you worship a dumb god, you'll be dumb. If you worship a god that has no life, you will be lifeless.

The person makes the image, then he trusts the image, he becomes like the image, and he misses the glory of the living God. Christians are the children of the living God. Your body, if you're a Christian, is the temple of the living God. Heaven is the city of the living God. The Holy Spirit is the Spirit of the living God. We have life because we trust the living God. God is not dead.

What does idolatry do to us? It gives us a false sense of security. An idolatrous person trusts in lies. He makes his own god and trusts in it, bows down and worships it. What does idolatry do to us? It makes us like the god that we worship.

I'm grateful that you and I, as Christians, can become like the God we worship. As we fellowship with the Lord Jesus Christ, as we meditate on the Word, as we worship Him, we become like Him. And, thank God, someday "we shall be like him; for we shall see him as he is" (I John 3:2).

What Idols Do People Have Today?

A third question is, What idols do people have today? It's rather unlikely that in the United States of America or Canada or any other nation that's been influenced by the Christian faith that people would actually carve stones or trees and make themselves gods. Idol worship is still going on, I'm sure, but we have more subtle idols today.

For example, some people make *other people* their idols. I read in I Corinthians 1 that some people in the church said, "Oh, I'm for Paul. Oh, I'm for Apollos. Oh, I'm for Cephas, or Peter" (see v. 12). They made other people their idols.

Some Christians idolize certain preachers. This is wrong. Do not fix your faith and your hope on any human being. Every preacher, great or otherwise, has feet of clay and will disappoint you. Some people look to others and make them their idols.

I sometimes get just a little bit nauseous when I see how the worldly crowd worships and emulates TV entertainers or Hollywood stars or even athletic stars. They worship them, and this is so dangerous. It's good to have our models. In the history of the United States of America we have a number of men who stand out as models of character and service, but we should not worship men and women as idols.

Some people live for *their body*. Their body is their god. In Philippians 3:19 Paul talked about people whose god is their belly, or appetite. They just live to satisfy their appetites. Romans 16:18 says, "For they that are such serve not our Lord Jesus Christ but their own body, and by good words and fair speeches deceive the hearts of the innocent." Some people simply worship their appetites, or their bodies.

We live in a pleasure-mad society, and everything is saturated with a carnal satisfaction. We see advertisements that tell us how to please the body, but we are neglecting the soul, the spiritual life. Some people worship *pleasure.* "This know, also, that in the last days perilous times shall come. For men shall be lovers of their own selves" (II Tim. 3:1,2). We're seeing that today. "Covetous"—that's idolatry. "Boasters, proud, blasphemers, disobedient to parents, unthankful, unholy, without natural affection [we're seeing that today], trucebreakers, false accusers, incontinent, fierce, despisers of those that are good, traitors, heady, high-minded, lovers of pleasures more than lovers of God" (vv. 2-4). I think this infection has gotten into the Church. "Lovers of pleasures"—if some television program is shown on a Sunday night, some people don't bother to go to the evening service. They just stay home and watch television—lovers of pleasures.

I meet people everywhere who deliberately stay away from church to see some baseball game or some other sporting event—lovers of pleasures more than lovers of God.

And then there are those who just live for *things.* "Covetousness (which is idolatry)," says Colossians 3:5. They live to accumulate things—more boats and more cars and more TV sets and more toys. "The only difference between men and boys is that men buy more expensive toys."

What idols do we have today? If you want to find out if you have idols in your life, here's a checklist. How can we detect the idols in our lives? There's the *devotion* test: For what are you working and living? There's the *dependence* test: What do you trust? When difficulties come, to what do you turn? There's the *delight* test: What gives you the most pleasure? There's the *decision* test: What guides you when you make your decisions? And there's the *destiny* test: What are you looking forward to?

What you worship and serve is what you are working for. What will you sacrifice for? That is your god. What will you change your plans for? That is your god. What are you trusting when difficulties come? That is your god. What gives you the greatest amount of pleasure? That is your god. We've got to be very careful that we do not have idols in our lives.

The Prophet Habakkuk ended chapter 2 by saying, "The Lord is in his holy temple; let all the earth keep silence before him" (v. 20).

Instead of a person's talking to a silent idol, we have a speaking God telling us to be silent. "Be still, and know that I am God" (Ps. 46:10).

The Lord is in His holy temple, and one day He will smash all of the idols. Do you know the living and the true God because you have trusted Jesus Christ as your Saviour? yes

ouch!

difficulties come what do you turn TO.

Replace all my Idols with only you - God

Chapter 10

The Prophet Prays

(Hab. 3:1,2)

In the third chapter of Habakkuk we find the prophet reaching the pinnacle of his spiritual experience. He is praising God from the heights!

In chapter 1 we found the prophet worrying and wondering. He was in the valley of despair, sighing and arguing with God. He had some problems with what God was doing in the world. He thought that God was indifferent and inactive. Then God told him what He was doing, and this raised the third problem. He thought God was inconsistent. He said, "God, how can You use the evil Babylonian nation to chastise Your people, the people of Judah?"

In chapter 2 he moved a little bit higher—he went up into his watchtower where he devoted himself to watching and waiting. He said, "I'm going to stand upon my watch, and I'm going to see what God is going to say to me and how He's going to answer me" (see v. 1). God answered him. God always does if we wait and watch.

He answered him by showing him the evil that existed in the Babylonian nation. God pronounced five woes upon the invading armies. But against this dark background of judgment and sin, God gave three very wonderful assurances: the assurance of His *grace*—"The just shall live by his faith" (v. 4); the assurance of His *glory*—"For the earth shall be filled with the knowledge of the glory of the Lord, as the waters cover the sea" (v. 14); and the assurance of His *government*—"But the Lord is in His holy temple; let all the earth keep silence before him" (v. 20).

In chapter 3 he moved from watching and waiting to worshiping and witnessing. We find the prophet on the heights, praising God! The book ends with verse 19: "The Lord God is my strength, and he will make my feet like hinds' feet, and he will make me walk upon mine high places." So Habakkuk started in the valley, but he ended up on the mountaintop! He started with sighing and ended with singing. He started with perplexity, and he ended with praise. How did all of this happen? He learned that the just shall live by faith.

When you come to chapter 3 of Habakkuk, you discover the prophet engaged in three activities. In verses 1 and 2 he is *praying*: "A prayer of Habakkuk, the prophet, upon Shigionoth." The word "Shigionoth" is a mystery to us. Some people think it refers to musical instruments. It's possible that Habakkuk was one of the levitical choir members in the temple, because the chapter ends, "To the chief singer on my stringed instruments" (v. 19). This musical notation would suggest that he was one of the musicians in the temple. Other scholars think that "Shigionoth" means an ecstatic kind of a statement—a statement, a prayer or a song with deep feeling. It really makes no difference, because the prayer is there for us to read regardless of what that word means. So in verses 1 and 2 we find the prophet praying.

Then in verses 3-15 Habakkuk is *pondering*. He is pondering the activity of God in history. "God came from Teman, and the Holy One from Mount Paran" (v. 3). Habakkuk meditated on the glory of God and the greatness of God in the history of the people of Israel.

In verses 16-19 Habakkuk is *praising*. It's a wonderful climax to this marvelous book as the prophet stands on his high places and praises God and says, "I'm going to trust God regardless of what may happen!"

Let's consider now his prayer given to us in verse 2: "O Lord, I have heard thy speech, and was afraid; O Lord, revive thy work in the midst of the years, in the midst of the years make known; in wrath remember mercy." As you consider this prayer, you will discover that it expresses three great concerns. He is concerned, first of all, about *God's Word*: "O Lord, I have heard thy speech, and was afraid." Then he is concerned about *God's work*: "O Lord, revive thy work in the midst of the years, in the midst of the years make known." Finally, he is concerned about *God's wrath:* "In wrath remember mercy."

Concerned About God's Word

Let's consider this first concern in Habakkuk 3:2. The prophet was concerned about God's Word: "O Lord, I have heard thy speech, and was afraid." He had heard the Word of God, but this was exactly what he wanted. In chapter 1 the prophet had questioned God and argued with God: "God, You are indifferent. God, You are inactive." Then God spoke to him and said, "I am not inactive. I am doing a marvelous work." Then the prophet argued with Him about that and said, "God, You are inconsistent." Then in chapter 2, verse 1, he said, "I'm going to stop arguing." That's a good thing to do—stop arguing with God. "I will stand upon my watch, and set myself upon the tower, and will watch to see what he will say unto me [what He shall answer concerning my complaint], and what I shall answer when I am reproved." He said, "I'm going to watch and wait and let God talk to me." help

It's marvelous when we learn to close our mouths and open our ears and listen for the voice of God. Every Christian should be able to say, "Speak, Lord; for thy servant heareth" (I Sam. 3:9). The prophet wanted to hear the Word of God, and God spoke to him. Habakkuk 2:2 says, "And the Lord answered me, and said," and then God spoke to him and told him about judgment and about His promises. So he heard the Word of God, which is what he wanted to do.

Hearing the Word generated faith. Faith doesn't come through feelings—faith comes through the

Word of God. "So, then, faith cometh by hearing, and hearing by the word of God" (Rom. 10:17). Now he was able to pray. The Word of God and prayer go together. "If ye abide in me, and my words abide in you, ye shall ask what ye will, and it shall be done unto you" (John 15:7). You cannot separate the Word of God from prayer, because prayer depends on faith, and faith depends on the Word of God. You cannot separate the Word of God and prayer, because the Word of God reveals the will of God, and prayer means asking in the will of God. You cannot separate the Word of God and prayer, because the Word of God gives us promises, and prayer depends on promises, not on explanations.

Habakkuk had power in prayer because he heard the Word of God. But when he heard the Word of God, he was troubled. "O Lord, I have heard thy speech, and was afraid" (Hab. 3:2). In fact, in verse 16 we are told how frightened he was. "When I heard, my belly trembled [my heart began to pound within me], my lips quivered at the voice; rottenness entered into my bones, and I trembled in myself, that I might rest in the day of trouble." When you look at the anatomy lesson we have here, it's rather interesting. His heart trembled, his lips quivered, his bones weakened, and his legs wobbled. That's what he said literally. From head to foot, the prophet was stirred by the Word of God. We don't see much of that today. We have people studying the Word of God but not stirred by the Word of God.

Help us

How much of the fear of the Lord comes to

people when the Word of God is read or proclaimed in your church assembly? How much of the fear of God comes to my life when I read the Word of God in my daily devotions? We mark the Bible, we study the Bible, we read the Bible, we even memorize the Bible, but we aren't always awestruck by the Bible. Daniel was. When Daniel heard the Word of God and saw the vision, he trembled. He became ill when God talked to him about prophetic events (see Dan. 7:15,28). I find people talking about prophetic events very glibly, and yet the visions that Daniel received made him ill.

In Isaiah 66:2 God says, "But to this man will I look, even to him that is poor and of a contrite spirit, and trembleth at my word." I read in Psalm 119:120: "My flesh trembleth for fear of thee, and I am afraid of thy judgments." Habakkuk was troubled at what he heard, and this was a good sign. It was proof that he really believed the Word of God.

His first concern in his prayer was God's Word. God had said to him in chapter 2, verse 4, "The just shall live by his faith." The prophet replied, "God, I'm going to believe Your Word." But believing the Word of God led to trembling in his heart.

Concern About God's Work

Habakkuk's second concern in his prayer was *God's work.* "O Lord, revive thy work in the midst of the years, in the midst of the years make known" (Hab. 3:2). What was God's work? God told him in 1:5,6: "Behold among the nations, and regard, and wonder marvelously; for I will work a work in your days, which ye will not believe, though it be told you. For, lo, I raise up the Chaldeans." That was God's work. Habakkuk had argued about this work and had told God He was making a mistake. But then he prayed, "Lord, keep this work going!"

The word "revive" in Habakkuk 3:2 has nothing to do with the modern revival meeting. The word "revive" means to "preserve alive, to keep going, to encourage." He prayed, "O God, keep alive this work that You are doing." In Habakkuk 1 the prophet was opposed to the Babylonians' coming. Later he said, "God, keep Your work going." Why? It was *God's* work. If it was God's work, it had to be good.

Why did he want this work to continue? He had realized that his people needed it. "We shall not die. O Lord, thou hast ordained them for judgment; and, O Mighty God, thou hast established them for correction" (v. 12). They were not coming for destruction; they were coming for discipline. They were not coming for condemnation; they were coming for correction. He said, "My people need correction. Now, God, keep this work going." Furthermore, Habakkuk not only wanted this work to be revived, but he wanted it to be made known. "Make known what You are doing" (see 3:2). This is exactly what God wanted done. "The Lord answered me, and said, Write the vision, and make it plain upon tablets, that he may run that readeth it" (2:2). Everyone who read what he had written should run and tell somebody else, "for the vision is yet for an appointed time, but at the end it shall speak, and not lie; though it tarry, wait for it, because it will surely come, it will not tarry" (v. 3).

The prophet wanted the Word of God and the work of God to be shared with everyone. This is the important task that God has given to the Church. What is the message that needs to go out? That there is a God of wrath who judges sin, but this God of judgment is also a God of grace. "The just shall live by his faith" (v. 4). If you will trust Jesus Christ as your Saviour, you don't have to be afraid of judgment.

Concerned About God's Wrath

He was concerned about God's Word and about God's work. And third, he was concerned about *God's wrath.* "In wrath remember mercy" (Hab. 3:2). The nation deserved wrath. All of the woes that were pronounced in Habakkuk 2 on the nation of Babylon could have been pronounced on the people of Judah. They were guilty of pride. They were guilty of selfish ambition and covetousness. They were guilty of exploiting one another. They were guilty of being addicted to strong drink, and they were surely guilty of idolatry. We like to see the sins of other people judged, but we don't want those same sins judged in our own lives.

The nation deserved wrath, but the prophet prayed, "In wrath remember mercy" (3:2). He was like Moses. When the nation of Israel sinned by worshiping the golden calf, Moses asked God for mercy (see Ex. 32). When the nation refused to believe God at Kadesh-Barnea and to enter into the

Promised Land, Moses asked God for mercy (see Num. 14).

Jeremiah the prophet was ministering about the same time as Habakkuk, and this is the way he prayed: "O Lord, I know that the way of man is not in himself; it is not in man that walketh to direct his steps. O Lord, correct me, but with justice; not in thine anger, lest thou bring me to nothing" (Jer. 10:23,24). Jeremiah was praying for mercy in the midst of judgment.

God did give mercy in the midst of judgment and wrath. In His justice He had to punish sin, but in His grace He provided for cleansing and forgiveness. After 70 years of captivity, the nation was restored to their land, and the temple was rebuilt. Then the walls were rebuilt, and the nation began to function again. Then the Saviour came and died outside the city of Jerusalem for the sins of the nation.

The prophet was praying, "O God, don't wait 70 years. In the midst of the years—right now—remember mercy." When God judges, He always judges in mercy. "He hath not dealt with us after our sins, nor rewarded us according to our iniquities" (Ps. 103:10).

God is at work today in mercy. These verses from Habakkuk are quoted in Acts 13:40,41: "Beware, therefore, lest that come upon you, which is spoken of in the prophets; behold, ye despisers, and wonder, and perish; for I work a work in your days, a work which ye shall in no way believe, though a man declare it unto you."

What was Paul talking about? The work of God's

grace: that God is saving Jews and Gentiles and bringing them together into one Body, the Church; that today is not a day of judgment, it's a day of mercy; that God has spoken in His Son and has sent Him to die for our sins. That is the message we want to proclaim. Pray that this message will prosper. Let's pray that God will revive the work He is doing in these years—the work of getting out the Gospel, of calling out a people for His name.

I trust that you are involved in some way, sacrificially, faithfully, in getting out the Word of God and accomplishing the work of God in this day.

Chapter 11

The Prophet Ponders

(Hab. 3:3-15)

The Prophet Habakkuk moved from *praying* to *pondering*. In chapter 3 of his little book, in the first two verses, we find him praying. But then in verses 3-15 we find him pondering. He is pondering the greatness and the glory of God as seen in the history of the Jewish people.

Praying is not just *asking* from God. Too many people have the idea that, when we pray, all we do is come and ask God for what we want or what we think we need. Prayer also involves seeing the glory of God. Prayer involves praising God for all that He is and all that He does. It's good for us, occasionally, to sit down and remember the greatness and the glory of God in all that He has done for us. In fact, one book in the Old Testament is devoted almost entirely to that theme—the Book of Deuteronomy. Over and over in that book, Moses said to the Jewish people, "Don't forget that you were slaves in Egypt. Don't forget what God did for you. Remember the Lord, your God. Remember all that He did for you and all that He is to you."

The Lord Jesus gave to the Church a supper of remembrance. The Lord's Supper is celebrated in remembrance of the Lord Jesus—to remind us that He died for us, to remind us that He's coming again.

So it is good for us as God's people to look back and remember the greatness and the glory of God as He has worked in our lives. When you get discouraged, when you feel as if God is not doing what He ought to do, just remember what He *has* done. "Bless the Lord, O my soul, and forget not all his benefits" (Ps. 103:2).

The circumstances around you change, but God does not change. The same God who helped you ten years ago can help you today. God does not change His principles, God does not change His promises, and God does not change His purposes. He may change His methods, and He may change His timing, but He never changes in His purposes, His principles or His promises. When you remember the mighty acts of God, you will be encouraged.

Let's do that now as we consider Habakkuk 3:3-15. This section is inspired poetry. It's really a hymn of praise to the greatness of God in history. Some people don't like poetry, and therefore they have a problem when they read a passage such as this in the Bible. Some truths have to be pictured. They are not explained, they are not spelled out to us in detail; rather, they are given to us in symbols. God can say some things to us better through picture-language, such as poetry, than in any other way.

This hymn of praise has three stanzas. In verses 3-5 he said, "God came." In verses 6 and 7, "God stood." And then in verses 8-15, "God marched." Those three statements, I think, would encourage me right now if I said nothing else. "God came"—He knows where I am, and He knows what my needs are. "God stood"—He didn't run away, He wasn't afraid. "God marched"—God went to work and took care of the enemy.

God Came

Stanza one says that *God came* (Hab. 3:3-5). "God came from Teman, and the Holy One from Mount Paran. Selah. His glory covered the heavens, and the earth was full of his praise. And his brightness was like the light; he had horns coming out of his hand; and there was the hiding of his power. Before him went the pestilence, and burning coals went forth at his feet."

Habakkuk started with a lesson on geography, and he takes us to that area in the south where the Jewish people had gone during their exodus and near Mount Sinai where God gave the Law. Parallel verses are Deuteronomy 33:2,3: "And he said, The Lord came from Sinai, and rose up from Seir unto them; he shined forth from Mount Paran, and he came with ten thousands of saints. From his right hand went a fiery law for them. Yea, he loved the people; all his saints are in thy hand: and they sat down at thy feet; every one shall receive of thy words." The opening stanza of Habakkuk's prayer reminds us of the God who descended at Mount Sinai and brought the Law.

The Holiness of God

The first emphasis is on the holiness of God: "The Holy One from Mount Paran" (Hab. 3:3). This is an important truth in the Book of Habakkuk. Habakkuk himself said in 1:12: "Art thou not from everlasting, O Lord, my God, mine Holy One?" Note also verse 13: "Thou art of purer eyes than to behold evil, and canst not look [with approval] on iniquity." The emphasis is on the holiness of God. Whatever God does is right because God is holy. God came in holiness.

The Glory of God

God came in glory. "His glory covered the heavens, and the earth was full of his praise" (Hab. 3:3). This reminds us of 2:14: "For the earth shall be filled with the knowledge of the glory of the Lord, as the waters cover the sea." The prophet saw the glory of God and the holiness of God.

He also heard the praise of God: "The earth was full of his praise" (3:3). The Babylonians were not praising God, and not many people in Judah were praising God, but all of nature was praising God. Even when men and women don't praise God, God's creation will always praise Him. "The heavens declare the glory of God, and the firmament showeth his handiwork" (Ps. 19:1). All of nature is praising God.

The Power of God

The power of God is also revealed here. "And his brightness was like the light" (Hab. 3:4). His brightness was like the splendor of the sunrise, which is beautiful. "He had horns [rays] coming out of his hand" (v. 4). It was as though lightning were flashing out from the hand of God. "And there was the hiding of his power" (v. 4). God sometimes hides His power. The prophet couldn't understand why God wasn't doing something to the people of Babylon. God said, "Don't be afraid, I have My power. It's right here in My hand." "Before him went the pestilence [plague]" (v. 5). This reminds us of the time when God went through the land of Egypt. "And burning coals [lightning] went forth at his feet" (v. 5). This is a marvelous, poetic picture of God's coming in His greatness and glory!

At the very beginning of this song of praise, as Habakkuk pondered the greatness of God, he saw a God of glory. He is a holy God, a glorious God, a God worthy of our praise, a God of power. His coming is like the splendor of the sunrise. His hands have rays of glory coming from them. Lightning flashes at His feet. What a marvelous picture!

There is nothing wrong with looking at geography and remembering God. I think sometimes we are so "ultraspiritual" we don't remember the blessing in the locations where God has done great things. When a Jew thought of Mount Sinai, he thought of the glory and the Law of God. We think of Calvary and the empty tomb. You can trace Abraham's life by the altars that he built and the names that he gave to the wells. When Jacob ran away from home, he came to Bethel, and Bethel became a very special place to him. There is nothing wrong with using human geography to remind yourself of spiritual blessings. There are some places in this world where you and I can go, and we are reminded of the blessing that God brought to us there. We don't worship the location, but we glorify the God who met us there.

Of course, God came to us in Jesus Christ. "The Word was made flesh, and dwelt among us" (John 1:14). When God came to us in Jesus Christ, He revealed His grace and His glory, and by trusting Christ we can be saved.

God Stood

In Habakkuk 3:6,7 is the second stanza of Habakkuk's prayer—*God stood.* "He stood, and measured the earth; he beheld, and drove asunder the nations; and the everlasting mountains were scattered, the perpetual hills did bow; his ways are everlasting. I saw the tents of Cushan in affliction: and the curtains of the land of Midian did tremble." God stood! God is unafraid. He comes to the earth and stands there, and He measures the nations. He is measuring for judgment. He is examining the nations. Some translations read: "He shook the earth." There He stands, and He beholds what is going on in the earth. He makes the earth tremble. The mountains crumble. The hills bow down. He is the Everlasting One. The armies of Cush and of Midian trembled as though they were in affliction.

The picture here is of God's standing and getting His army ready to move. The prophet was remembering when Israel marched out of Egypt and went through the wilderness and then entered the land of Canaan. When Israel marched, the other nations trembled because God's people were coming.

This says to me, "Don't be afraid. God is standing near. Don't worry about what God may be doing. He knows what He's doing." God came, and God stood.

God Marched

Then *God marched* (Hab. 3:8-15). We see God on the move. "Thou didst march through the land in indignation; thou didst thresh the nations in anger" (v. 12). Let's follow God's march, for this is the picture of a great conqueror's moving on from victory to victory. Habakkuk the prophet saw the Babylonians on the march, moving from victory to victory. Then he pondered the greatness of God. God was on the march, and nothing could stop Him.

"Was the Lord displeased against the rivers? Was thine anger against the rivers? Was thy wrath against the sea, that thou didst ride upon thine horses and thy chariots of salvation?" (v. 8). Here we have the opening of the Red Sea for the Jewish nation. The chariots of Egypt went down in the water and the mud, and the soldiers were drowned. When Israel got to the Jordan River, the Jordan opened up for them. God marched ahead and opened up the way.

God can do that for you. When the child of God is

in the will of God, he can expect God to open the way for him.

"Thy bow was made quite naked [He uncovered His weapons], according to the oaths of the tribes, even thy word" (v. 9). God called for many arrows to be shot. "Thou didst cleave the earth with rivers" (v. 9). He knew where the water was. "The mountains saw thee, and they trembled; the overflowing of the water passed by; the deep uttered its voice, and lifted up its hands on high" (v. 10). Time after time God used the rain or the water to accomplish His purposes. "The sun and moon stood still in their habitation" (v. 11). This reminds us of Joshua 10. "At the light of thine arrows they went, and at the shining of thy glittering spear" (Hab. 3:11). God's armies, as they moved forth, shot their arrows and threw their spears, and they were like lightning. "Thou didst march through the land in indignation" (v. 12). Now we have the people of Israel conquering Canaan. "Thou didst thresh the nations in anger" (v. 12). Patiently God had waited for these heathen nations to repent, and they refused to. Now the time of judgment had come. "Thou wentest forth for the salvation of thy people, even for salvation with thine anointed" (v. 13). God's anointed people were experiencing the salvation of God, and the Lord brought about that salvation.

God is still doing that. It may look to us as though God isn't doing anything, but He is working for His anointed people, His covenant remnant. He's working for those who belong to Him.

Habakkuk saw, in verses 13-15, the conquest of

Babylon. "Thou woundedst the head out of the house of the wicked, by laying bare the foundation unto the neck" (v. 13). Some translations read: "You stripped him from head to foot" or "You laid bare his bones." In other words, the great people of Babylon who were sweeping through the land, laying everything bare, stripping the forest, killing the animals, wiping out the towns and villages—one day *they* would be stripped from head to foot.

"Thou didst strike through with his own staves the head of his villages; they came out like a whirlwind to scatter me; their rejoicing was as if to devour the poor secretly" (v. 14). But instead it was God who devoured them.

This is a marvelous hymn as Habakkuk pondered the greatness and the glory of God. God came. There is going to be a time when God is going to come in judgment. God stood. God is going to measure His enemy and say, "All right, I am now coming to meet you." And God marched. One of these days He's going to march through with judgment. The tragedy is that most people aren't prepared for God to come in judgment. Most people don't know Jesus as their Saviour. And that's why it's important for us to get the message out.

You'll notice that when he finished pondering the greatness of God, the prophet had a twofold response. One was *fear*: "When I heard, my belly trembled" (v. 16). Literally, that means, "My heart pounded, my innermost being was all shook up." "My lips quivered at the voice; rottenness entered into my bones, and I trembled in myself" (v. 16). So his first response was one of fear. His second response was that of *faith*. He praised God and affirmed his confidence in God, come what may!

No matter what your situation is today, look to God. Don't look at your circumstances, look to God. Remember what God has done for you. Review His past wonders. God came and God stood and God marched, and God can and will do this again. So don't be afraid, and don't complain. Just trust Him. And one day you will say, " 'I will rejoice in the Lord, I will joy in the God of my salvation' (v. 18)."

Chapter 12

The Prophet Praises God

(Hab. 3:16-19)

The Prophet Habakkuk has now reached the glorious climax of his experience with God. In chapter 3 he began by *praying*. Then he continued by *pondering* the greatness of God. In verses 16-19 we find him *praising* the Lord, praising God as the result of his praying and his pondering. And to think that all of this experience began in chapter 1 with the prophet's having problems with God!

God does not turn away from those who have honest questions. He does not answer those who are merely curious, but He does answer those who sincerely come to Him with a broken and a concerned heart.

Habakkuk faced reality. He couldn't understand what God was doing. He told God about it, and God met his needs. Habakkuk learned what we need to learn—that we don't live on explanations; we live on promises.

He faced the reality of his situation. He looked within in verse 16 and discovered that he was falling apart: "When I heard, my belly trembled, my lips quivered at the voice; rottenness entered into my bones, and I trembled in myself." His heart was trembling, his lips were quivering, his bones were weakening, his legs were wobbling, and there he stood, having heard the word of the living God. He had seen this marvelous vision of God, and it had affected him deeply.

He looked around, and everything around him was falling apart. Verse 17 says, "Although the fig tree shall not blossom, neither shall fruit be in the vines; the labor of the olive shall fail, and the fields shall yield no food; the flock shall be cut off from the fold, and there shall be no herd in the stalls." The economy was falling apart. You expect that in war, don't you?

Babylon would be violent when its armies moved in. "For the violence of Lebanon shall cover thee" (2:17). They would strip the forest. "The spoil of beasts, which made them afraid, because of men's blood, and for the violence of the land, of the city, and of all that dwell therein" (v. 17). Because of the invasion, everything would be destroyed.

Habakkuk 3:17 mentions the basic ingredients of life for the Jewish people: the figs, the vines, the olives, the fields, the flocks, the herds. Habakkuk said, "The shelves on the market are empty, but I'm still going to rejoice in the Lord, and I will joy in the God of my salvation" (see vv. 17,18). When you look within and discover you are falling apart, and when you look around and see that everything is falling to pieces, the only thing to do is *to look up and to trust God.* That's exactly what he did. "Yet I will rejoice in the Lord, I will joy in the God of my salvation" (v. 18).

This is an amazing paragraph in the Word of God. It's one of the greatest statements of faith found anywhere. Habakkuk said, in effect, "I can see the army coming. They are going to wipe everything out." We could put this in everyday language: "Although the stock market might collapse and no jobs are listed in the newspaper, although no food is on the shelves in the supermarket and everything is closed down because nobody has any money, although everything is falling apart, I will still rejoice in the Lord. I will joy in the God of my salvation."

It is amazing that the prophet should have such tremendous faith! He didn't start that way. He started in chapter 1 with a great deal of questioning and doubting. He was wondering and worrying. But now he is worshiping and witnessing because he has learned to live by faith.

"I Will Rest in God"

Habakkuk gave three marvelous affirmations of faith. In spite of the way he felt and in spite of what he saw going on in the economy, he said, *"I will rest in God."* "I trembled in myself, that I might rest in the day of trouble. When he cometh up unto the people, he will invade them with his troops" (Hab. 3:16).

What was "the day of trouble"? The "day of trouble" was the day when Babylon would be judged. The day was going to come when God would judge Babylon. "Now," said the prophet, "I will rest in the Lord. I will rest in the Lord in spite of the fact that my heart has been trembling."

Has your heart ever beat against your rib cage because of fear and concern? The prophet said, "My heart has been trembling, but I will rest in God." He saw Babylon's judgment coming. "I can wait patiently. The day will come when God will judge Babylon." He knew God was at work.

In chapter 1 God had said, "I am working a work in this world" (see v. 5). This is the equivalent of Romans 8:28: "And we know that all things work together for good to them that love God, to them who are the called according to his purpose." Romans 8:28 doesn't say that we will *see* all things working together for good. It doesn't say we will *feel* that all things are working together for good. It says we *know* it. How do we know it? God said so.

I think too many Christians believe that Romans 8:28 is telling us what we should see or what we should feel. No, it tells us what we should know. And in spite of the fact that he looked around and saw all kinds of trouble, the Prophet Habakkuk said, "I will rest in God. I know God is at work."

He said, "I will rest in God because He has told me to wait, and I will wait." "For the vision is yet for an appointed time, but at the end it shall speak, and not lie; though it tarry, wait for it, because it will surely come, it will not tarry" (Hab. 2:3). This is a good word to us. I have a hard time waiting. When I'm in a line at the airport or somewhere else, I can't figure out why everybody is so slow. I want to keep on the move, and God often says to me, "Now, wait, just wait, I am at work." Through faith and patience we inherit the promises. "Wait on the Lord; . . . and he shall strengthen thine heart. Wait, I say, on the Lord" (Ps. 27:14).

So Habakkuk said that he could rest in the Lord because he knew that one day God would judge the enemy. He could rest in the Lord because he knew God was at work. And he could rest in the Lord because God had told him to wait. His faith was at such a place that he *could* trust God and just wait.

It's marvelous when the believer can rest in God in spite of the way he feels. "My heart is trembling, my lips are quivering, my bones are weakened, my legs are wobbling, but I will rest in God."

Do you have that kind of rest? Jesus said, "Come unto me, all ye that labor and are heavy laden, and I will give you rest. Take my yoke upon you, and learn of me; for I am meek and lowly in heart, and ye shall find rest unto your souls" (Matt. 11:28,29). By faith, we can rest in God.

"I Will Rejoice in God"

Habakkuk's second affirmation of faith was *"I will rejoice in God"* (see Hab. 3:18). "Though the fig tree shall not blossom, and all the vines on the olive tree fail, though there be no crops in the field, though the flocks and the herds are all slaughtered, yet I will rejoice in the Lord. I will joy in the God of my salvation" (see vv. 17,18).

Previous to this his lips had been trembling and quivering. "My lips quivered at the voice" (v. 16). But now his lips were opened in praise. He was rejoicing in God. He could not rejoice in his circumstances. War is brutal. The Babylonians were going to swoop down upon Judah and do terrible things. Read the Book of the Lamentations of Jeremiah and find out how awful the invasion was. He could not rejoice in his circumstances, but he could rejoice in the God who is *above* our circumstances. You can always rejoice in God.

I notice here that he said God was his strength, his salvation and his song. "I will rejoice in the Lord, I will joy [the song] in the God of my salvation [the salvation]. The Lord God is my strength" (vv. 18,19). The Lord God was his strength, his song and his salvation. That refrain goes all the way through the Old Testament Scriptures. The first time you find it is in Exodus 15. Moses and the Children of Israel, on the other side of the Red Sea, were singing a song of victory. "The Lord is my strength and song, and he is become my salvation" (v. 2). So Israel sang that when they were delivered from Egypt.

When Israel went into captivity, they lost their song (Ps. 137), but after 70 years they came back from captivity and started to sing again. Psalm 118 was probably sung at the dedication of the restored temple. Verse 14 says, "The Lord is my strength and song, and is become my salvation." So Israel sang this song when they were delivered from Babylon.

Isaiah 12 says that the day is coming when God will restore His people to their land. He will open up a way for them to go back. Isaiah 12:2 says,

"Behold, God is my salvation; I will trust, and not be afraid; for the Lord, even the Lord [Jehovah], is my strength and my song; he also is become my salvation."

In Exodus 15:2, Psalm 118:14 and Isaiah 12:2 we hear the same refrain. Habakkuk also sang it. "Even though I cannot rejoice in my circumstances, I can rejoice in God. He is my song, He is my salvation, and He is my strength."

You can always rejoice in the Lord. Paul wrote to the Philippians: "Rejoice in the Lord always; and again I say, Rejoice" (Phil. 4:4). You can rejoice in what the Lord is. You can rejoice in what the Lord has done and in what He will do. You can rejoice in all that He is to you. You can always rejoice in the Lord, even if you can't rejoice in the land. The prophet saw everything in the land falling apart, but he was still able to rejoice in the Lord.

As you look around and see everything falling apart and you wonder what's going to happen next, can you say, "I will rest in God"? Can you say, "I will rejoice in God"?

"I Will Rely on God"

Habakkuk's third affirmation of faith was *"I will rely on God"* (see Hab. 3:19). In verse 16 he said that his legs were wobbling and his bones were shaking, but now he could say, "I'm going to rely on God. He is my strength." It makes no difference if my heart is trembling; I can *rest* in God. If my lips are quivering, I can *rejoice* in God. If my legs are shaking and my bones are breaking, I can *rely* on God. "The Lord God is my strength, and he will make my feet like hinds' feet" (v. 19), like the feet of the deer, able to run swiftly and surely. Sometimes God turns us into eagles. "They that wait upon the Lord shall renew their strength; they shall mount up with wings like eagles" (Isa. 40:31). Sometimes when there is difficulty, God gives us the grace and the faith to soar above it. Sometimes He turns us into lovely deer that are swift and sure as they run on the mountains.

The prophet's experience began down in the valley in chapter 1. Then he moved to the watchtower in chapter 2. But in chapter 3 he was running swiftly on the mountains. "He will make me walk upon mine high places" (v. 19).

What does it mean to walk upon high places? In the Bible it means to live in victory. Deuteronomy 32:13 says, "He made him ride on the high places of the earth, that he might eat the increase of the fields; and he made him to suck honey out of the rock, and oil out of the flinty rock." Deuteronomy 32 explains how God led Israel from victory to victory. When you are on the high places, you are living in victory and praising God.

You and I as Christians are living in the heavenly places (see Eph. 2:6). Our names are written down in heaven. Our Father is in heaven. Our home is in heaven. Our treasures are in heaven. Our hope is in heaven. Our Saviour is in heaven. Everything that we know is important is in heaven.

The prophet was saying, "I will rely on God. I am

not going to run away. I am going to go higher and higher." That is a marvelous statement of faith.

In Habakkuk 3:18 he said, "I will rejoice in the Lord [jump for joy], I will joy in the God of my salvation." The word "joy" means "I will spin around." In chapter 1 Habakkuk was gloomy and ready to quit, but here he was jumping for joy and spinning around for joy. Why? Because he knew that God was going to take care of everything.

Can you make these affirmations today? Is this your praise—"I will rest in God, I will rejoice in God, I will rely on God"? Are you still living in chapter 1 of Habakkuk, worrying and wondering? Or are you in chapter 2, watching and waiting? Why don't you move to chapter 3 by faith and start worshiping and witnessing? By faith you can be worshiping and witnessing and enjoying the heights with the Lord. You can trust in Him. "The just shall live by his faith" (2:4).